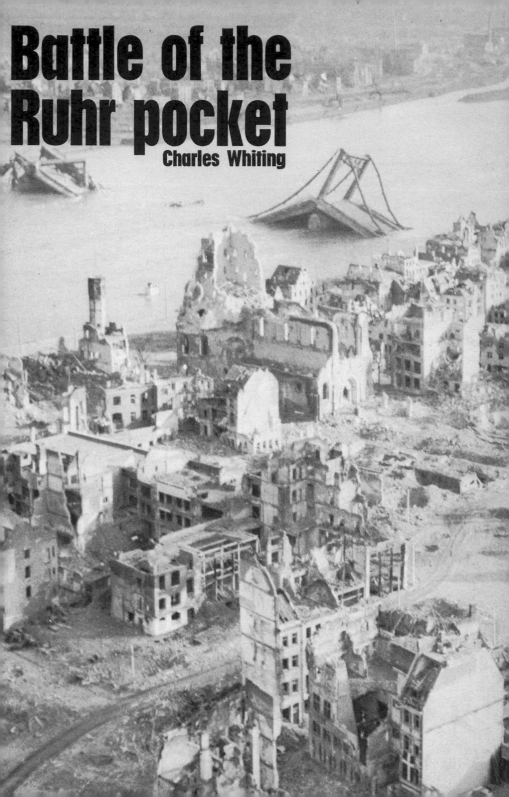

Battle of the
Ruhr pocket
Charles Whiting

Pan/Ballantine

Editor-in-Chief: Barrie Pitt
Editor: David Mason
Art Director: Sarah Kingham
Picture Editor: Robert Hunt
Designer: Michael Fry
Cover: Denis Piper
Special Drawings: John Batchelor
Photographic Research: Nan Shuttleworth
Cartographer: Richard Natkiel

First U.S. Printing: February, 1971
First Pan/Ballantine Printing: February, 1972

Printed in United States of America

Ballantine Books, Ltd.—An Intertext Publisher
Pan Books, Ltd.
33 Tothill Street, London, S.W. 1

Contents

The great decision

Introduction by Peter Elstob

Something strange seemed to happen to General Eisenhower in the closing weeks of the Second World War. On 28th March, without informing the Joint Chiefs of Staff or the British Prime Minister, he sent a personal message to Stalin which was a major change in grand strategy – the Western Allies would not advance to Berlin to meet the Russians but would 'effect a junction' along a line running through Erfurt-Leipzig-Dresden.

Only the day before Field-Marshal Montgomery had told General Eisenhower that his 21st Army Group were about to drive hard for the line of the river Elbe so as to gain possession of the plains of northern Germany from which a rapid advance to Berlin would be possible. Now Eisenhower sent a directive to Montgomery saying that as soon as the Ruhr was encircled Ninth United States Army would be taken away from him and used for mopping up the Ruhr and that 21st Army Group would be used to protect 12th Army Group's (Bradley's) northern flank as they made the main thrust south east.

This decision to make the main Allied advance from the centre towards Dresden instead of from the left towards Berlin and to wait until the Ruhr was clear of German troops has been hotly debated by historians for the last twenty-five years. It may have been that seeing victory so clearly within his grasp the Supreme Commander, a humane man, wanted to keep casualties down – General Bradley had warned that an assault on Berlin would cost a hundred thousand men – or perhaps, with the memory of the totally unexpected great German Ardennes Offensive still fresh in his mind he was reluctant to push forward without securing his flanks against another such German assault which, though it could certainly not succeed, would prove most costly to defeat. Undoubtedly too the spectre of fanatical German soldiers selling their lives dearly defending the 'National Redoubt' in south Bavaria, conjured up by SHAEF Intelligence, loomed large in his thinking. Then again there was the simple military fact that the Russians already had a million soldiers poised forty miles from Berlin while his forces were 200 miles away, a situation which made it extremely unlikely that he could beat them to Berlin anyway.

Although all these factors weighed with Eisenhower there were two other reasons for the dramatic decision which dissipated the enormous Allied forces along a broad front instead of concentrating them in a single hard thrust as had been originally planned. First General Eisenhower had finally become convinced that Field-Marshal Montgomery would not plunge ahead like General Bradley who, Eisenhower said, 'has never paused to regroup when he saw an opportunity to advance'. The second reason was the effect of the disunity which had been brought about in his command by the bitterness of the rivalries, the extent of the jealousies and the shortsightedness of the competition among his subordinate generals.

Marshal Foch said that his experience in the First World War had caused him to lose much of his veneration for Napoleon, for the Little Corporal had always fought coalitions and any reasonably efficient general could defeat a coalition. By 1945 General Eisenhower would have ruefully agreed.

Among the bitterest rivalries was that which had grown up between Montgomery and Bradley after the Ardennes Offensive but this was by no means the only one. Patton was convinced that he was fighting SHAEF, First Army and the British as well as the Germans, the French were certain that the intention was to squeeze them out of the final offensive and Ninth Army believed that Second Army wanted all the credit for crossing the Lower Rhine. While the Allied armies were waiting to cross the Rhine one of Patton's men in Antwerp chalked 'Third Army' on every mobile bridge that was landed. Only because First Army had learned from bitter experience did they take the precaution of having one of their men at Liège rubbing out 'Third' and writing 'First'.

By the time the defeat of the Germans had become a certainty some of Eisenhower's most senior commanders were fighting their own war, a war in which prestige, national or otherwise, was considered more important than the quick defeat of the enemy. For all these reasons General Eisenhower decided against leaving the Ruhr forces to be contained by a reinforced Fifteenth Army while the experienced British, American and French soldiers of the 21st, 12th and 6th Army Groups bypassed the area and smashed their way eastward as far and as fast as possible. Instead more than half the divisions in Ninth and First Armies became embroiled for two very important weeks in the gigantic mopping-up operation which is the subject of this book.

The Ruhr Pocket, the largest double envelopment in history, exceeded both Stalingrad and Tunisia in the number of prisoners taken, and the list of surrendered divisions and captured generals reads like a roll call of Germany's best. Casualties were surprisingly low because of the state of morale in the weary, battered Wehrmacht, most of whose members only wanted the senseless war to come to an end. Some units however, greatly outnumbered, left without air cover to the mercy of the fighter-bombers, were able to scrape up a few tanks or self-propelled guns and fought with a zeal and ferocity which was almost unbelievable at that stage of the war. The Americans, by then battle-hardened soldiers, went about their work with determination and efficiency.

The battle of the Ruhr had its moments of tragedy on the grand scale, moments of high comedy, acts of great heroism and sudden, understandable collapse. Charles Whiting has skilfully captured them all in this first detailed and complete history of the battle which resulted in completely breaking the power of the Germans to carry on the war on the Western Front.

Thrust across the Rhine

The River Rhine, which had not been crossed by force since the days of Napoleon, had long been considered the last and greatest natural barrier to the heart of Germany by the Allies. For months the western planners had been preparing for the day when they would have to cross it. But never once during that period had they ever considered that they would find a bridge across the mighty waterway intact. But in the first week of March 1945 that seemingly fantastic possibility appeared as if it might be realised.

On 2nd March, the 83rd Division of the US Ninth Army discovered that there was an intact bridge some

fifteen miles away in the neighborhood of Düsseldorf. With German-speaking soldiers in the lead and with their tanks camouflaged to look like German vehicles, the Americans passed boldly through the enemy lines and started full pelt for the bridge. But they were challenged by a lone German soldier, a member of a small German column. The Americans easily wiped out the enemy in the ensuing fire fight. But the noise warned the defenders of the bridge, and as the first US tanks lumbered to its approaches, the Düsseldorf bridge went up in the air.

One day later the US 2nd Armored Division of the same army came even closer to seizing a bridge across the Rhine. Fifteen miles north of Düsseldorf, the leading units of the division found themselves confronted with the huge three-span *Adolf Hitler Brücke*, some 1,600 feet long. Two officers actually crossed the bridge to the other side and got back to tell their tale to the commander of the American task force, which tried for almost one day to take the enormous structure by a *coup de main*. But in the end the *Adolf Hitler Brücke* suffered the same fate as the other Düsseldorf bridge. The Germans exploded it in the Americans' faces.

Of all the Rhine bridges still standing in that first week of March –

and there were not many left by then – the Ludendorff railway bridge at the little German town of Remagen, just below Bonn, was considered the least desirable by the Allies. It had never once been mentioned in the months of planning that had gone into the consideration of where the Allies would cross the mighty waterway. The eastern bank presented an excellent defensive position with the cliffs around the east side of the bridge rising to 600 feet. In addition, the area was heavily wooded and the roads few and of poor quality. Remagen was not thought of as an ideal place to launch an armoured breakout. However General Hodges of the US First Army had briefly discussed the possibility of capturing the bridge with General Millikin of his III Corps, which was approaching the general area of Remagen. But both men had concluded on that fourth day of March that the possibility was pretty remote that the bridge would still be intact when Millikin's Corps reached the Rhine.

General von Zangen, commander of the German Fifteenth Army, which was holding a section of the front twenty-five miles west of Remagen, was not so sure. He knew his neighbour the Fifth Panzer Army, badly battered a few months earlier in the Ardennes, had retreated to the Rhine, leaving a sixty-mile gap between the two armies, and he had an uncanny feeling that the Americans might burst through and seize the bridge. He told Field-Marshal Model, the commander of Army Group B and the overall chief of that section of the front, of his fears. But Model dismissed his fears. Only a fool, he told Zangen, would try to cross the Rhine at such a spot, and he forbade the Fifteenth Army Com-

Above: Lieutenant-General Hodges, commanding US First Army. *Left:* The Adolf Hitler bridge, like many others, blown up in the face of the Allied advance

mander to send any troops to the rear to defend the bridge.

But even while that conversation between the two German commanders was taking place the armoured spearheads of General Hodges' US First Army were hurrying towards the Rhine with other intentions than seizing the Remagen bridge. Headed by the 9th Armored Division, the drive was aimed at linking up with Patton's Third Army coming up the left bank of the Moselle in the direction of Koblenz, and in a great pincer movement trapping all the Germans, including Zangen's Fifteenth Army, west of the Rhine between Koblenz and Cologne.

By the afternoon of 6th March the 9th Armored had already penetrated the gap between the Fifteenth and Fifth German Armies and with General Hoge's Combat Command B

in the lead was rolling into the little country town of Meckenheim, some twelve miles from Remagen. While Hodges paused in Mechenheim to regroup and wait for orders, his divisional commander General Leonard requested the division's mission from General Millikin. During the course of the conversation, the Corps Commander remarked casually: 'Do you see that little black strip of bridge at Remagen? If you happen to get that, your name will go down in glory.' But still no firm decision was made about capturing the Ludendorff Bridge.

On the morning of 7th March General Hoge divided his combat command into two teams: one to cross the River Ahr at Sinzig; the other under Colonel Engeman to take the town of Remagen. Engeman got off to a late start because the damage to the town

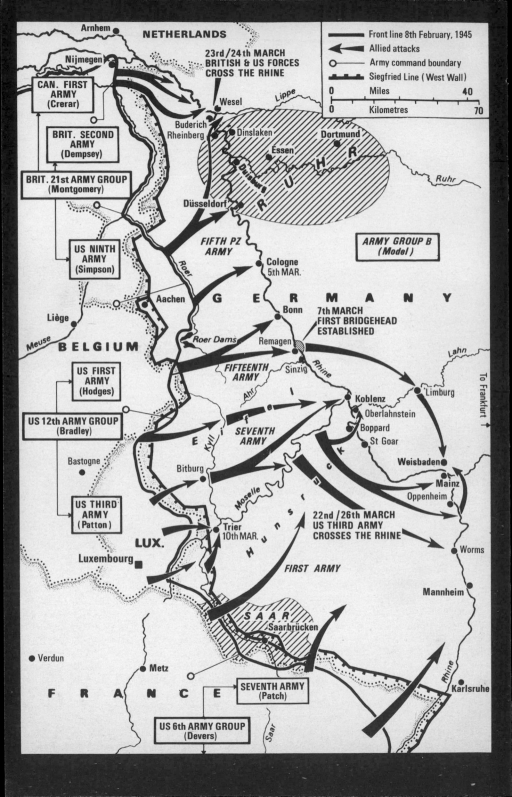

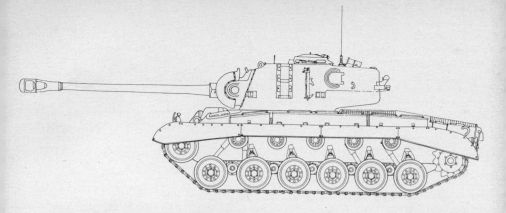

The American M26 Pershing arrived in Europe just in time to see some combat before the end of the war. Designed after a series of pilot models with differing armament and transmission, the M26 was designed to replace the projected M6 series, which had been rejected, among other reasons, because it was too difficult to transport on account of its considerable weight. The M26 had a low silhouette for a tank of its size. *Crew :* Five. *Weight :* 41 tons. *Armament :* one 90mm gun, two .3-inch and one .5-inch machine guns. *Ammunition :* 70 rounds of 90mm, 5,000 rounds of .3-inch and 550 rounds of .5-inch. *Speed :* 20mph on roads, 5mph cross country. *Range :* 92 miles maximum. *Armour :* 4-inch upper nose and turret front, 3-inch hull and turret sides and turret rear, 2-inch hull upper rear and 1-inch turret roof. *Length :* 28 feet 10 inches. *Width :* 11 feet 6 inches. *Height :* 9 feet 1 inch

of Meckenheim held up his progress, but finally at 8.20 am one company of armoured infantry and a platoon of the new Pershing tanks armed with 90mm guns were on the road to Remagen.

Roughly five hours later the team reached the heights to the west of the Rhine and saw the silver snake of the river below, and with it – the bridge! For a moment or two, the Americans believed it was some kind of trap, but Colonel Engeman did not hestiate. He informed his men that they were going down. General Hodges, who reached the scene some time later, confirmed Engeman's decision, but added new urgency to the proceedings by crying: 'Grab that bridge!' Turning to Engeman, he said, 'Take some tanks and put them on each side of it and fire across the river. Send your infantry across when you establish fire superiority.'

Feverishly the Germans on the other side tried to explode the charges

which would destroy the bridge, but they were blinded by the phosphorus smoke which the Americans were laying down all about them and became utterly confused. Then Captain Bratge, in temporary command of the bridge, discovered that the detonator did not work. A crew was sent out to do the job with 300 kilograms of explosive and although they succeeded in exploding their charges, when the smoke cleared the bridge was still intact and the Americans were beginning to move across.

By 4.30 pm that same day, the bridge had been cleared of explosives and III Corps had been committed to 'throw everything it had' across to the far side. Some time later Hodges, First Army Commander, telephoned General Bradley, Commander of the 12th US Army Group to which the First Army belonged. Bradley was in conference with General Bull, Eisenhower's G-3, and when the latter heard the dramatic news, he replied unenthusiastically, 'Sure you've got a bridge, Brad, but what good is it going to do you? You're not going anywhere down there at Remagen. It just doesn't fit into the plan'.

Hotly Bradley retorted, 'A bridge is a bridge and mighty damn good anywhere across the Rhine!'

Bull remained unconvinced. He knew that Allied strategy for the Rhine called for a crossing of the river by Montgomery's 21st Army Group north of the Ruhr. His lack of enthusiasm showed itself on his somewhat pudgy face and an angry Bradley cried: 'What in hell do you want us to do, pull back and blow it up?'

Bull did not answer so Bradley called Eisenhower at his HQ at Rheims to tell him of the unexpected capture and confirm the unofficial approval he had given to Hodges' III Corps crossing of the river. Eisenhower, unlike Bull, was delighted by the news. As he records the event in his memoirs: 'I could scarcely believe my ears. He and I had frequently discussed the development as a remote possibility but never a well-founded hope. I fairly shouted into the telephone: 'How much have you got in that vicinity that you can throw across the river?'

Bradley then confessed he had committed a corps and Eisenhower replied, 'Go ahead and shove at least five divisions across and anything else necessary to make certain of your hold.'

The capture of the Remagen Bridge was, as Eisenhower confessed three years later, 'one of my happy moments of the war', and although to a certain extent it interfered with Montgomery's intended crossing in the north, he encouraged Bradley to expand the First Army's bridgehead on the other side. Thus while Montgomery prepared for his massive, full-scale crossing in two weeks' time, Hodges persisted in building up the bridgehead. To his rear the Germans tried desperately to destroy the bridge. They used long-range artillery,

frogmen armed with explosives, bombers, rockets, floating mines, all without success, and when finally the bridge collapsed of its own accord, on 17th March, the Americans already had a heavy duty 'Treadway bridge' across and their supply route secured. By that time the First Army had by means of piecemeal yet continual attacks extended its bridgehead ten miles northeast through difficult country, and the US 9th Infantry Division was coming ever closer to its objective, the Frankfurt-Cologne autobahn.

Now it was up to Montgomery to secure the major crossing of the river upon which the strategy of the remaining weeks of the war depended. The British part in Operation Plunder,

Above left: Field-Marshal Model, commanding Army Group B
Above right: Brigadier-General Hoge. *Below:* The Ludendorf rail bridge at Remagen left for a time substantially intact after a German attempt to destroy it

the 21st Army Group's crossing of the Rhine, has been described often enough. It entailed a crossing of the river near Wesel by two infantry divisions and a commando brigade, followed some time later, once the opposite shore had been secured, by the daylight landing of airborne troops, both British and American. Here we are more concerned with the assault of the US Ninth Army, which was subsequently to play a vital role in the Ruhr Pocket fighting.

The Ninth Army's assault was made by the XVI Corps by the 30th and 79th Divisions. One division crossed the river north of Rheinberg (south of Wesel) and another attacked east of the town. Along the eight-mile two-divisional front, the Americans were faced by the German 180th and Hamburg Divisions.

The 30th Division committed all of its three regiments, each sending a battalion across near Buderich, Wallach and Rheinberg. Machine-guns fired tracer ahead of the lead assault boats to guide the first wave. Quickly the first group of infantry hit the far bank of the river, scrambled up the dike and had captured it virtually before they had realised what they had achieved. As one company commander remarked 'There was no real fight to it. The artillery had done the job for us.'

One hour later two regiments of the 79th Division started their assault. At first there was some confusion because of the smoke which had been laid to cover the crossing sites, but after this had been overcome, the infantry speedily reached the other side against very light opposition.

By mid-morning the Ninth Army was able to start ferrying tanks across, and as dusk descended that same day the Ninth had captured its first objective, Dinslaken, and gained

The Remagen bridge. *Left above:* Troops shelter before advancing across.
Left: Safe arrival on the other side of the Rhine

17

Above: The weakened Remagen bridge collapses; a pontoon bridge is ready to carry traffic. *Below:* Allied Airborne Army troops concentrate near Wesel

Lieutenant-General Omar N Bradley, 12th Army Group Commander

Major-General Harold R Bull, Assistant Chief of Staff, SHAEF

the distinction of completing the first bridge across the Rhine in that area; a 1,150 foot Treadwell, built in record time by 4.20 pm. In the words of the US official historian 'the 9th had crossed perhaps the most imposing water obstacle in Western Europe at a cost of thirty-one casualties.'

Meanwhile on 24th March Patton's Third Army started to participate in the assaults on the Rhine. Already Patton, hoping to make Montgomery's much vaunted crossing look a little ridiculous, had two days earlier sneaked an infantry division across the great river at Oppenheim; now he ordered General Middleton's VIII Corps to cross between Boppard and St Goar.

The Rhine between these two towns was an unlikely spot for a successful crossing. The river flows through a deep canyon, with the shore on the far bank reaching up between 300 and 400 feet in almost sheer cliffs. Moreover the eastern bank was well defended

by Höhne's LXXXIV Corps which had some 400 infantry, an anti-aircraft brigade, ten howitzers, and a mixed bag of policemen, *Volkssturm* units and remnants from several other formations dug in along the shoreline.

All the same Middleton set about his task with a will. Just before midnight on 24th March his 87th Division sent across four battalions of infantry. Near Rhens one of these battalions came under such heavy enemy fire that it took an hour to get across. But a few hundred yards down stream another of the 87th's battalions crossed completely unopposed until it struck the opposite shore. One day later these crossing sites near Rhens were abandoned in favour of those gained by the two other battalions at Boppard, where the attack had gone in without difficulty so that the American infantry had been able to move forward and capture Oberlahnstein at the confluence of the Rivers Lahn and Rhine.

Three days later, on 28th March,

Top left: Operation Plunder; British troops prepare to cross the Rhine at dawn
Centre left: Artillery fires to support the crossing near Rhineburg
Bottom left: Ninth Army troops make the Rhineburg crossing. *Above:* Patton (right) discusses future moves with Major-General Eddy, near Oppenheim

the Allied armies in the West had successfully established their bridge-heads all along the Rhine. In the north the Americans under Montgomery had experienced hard fighting against a stiffening German resistance, but by now they had closed on the built-up areas of the Ruhr from the Rhine to Sterkade and cleared most of the wooded area north from there up to the Lippe Canal. For the cost of 3,968 British and 2,813 American casualties, the 21st Army Group had a bridgehead with a breadth of thirty-five miles and a depth of twenty.

At the Remagen bridgehead Hodges' First Army had at last received the green light to break out from Eisenhower and now one of its arm-oured columns was streaking through the German defences and heading down the Ruhr-Frankfurt autobahn in the direction of Limburg and beyond towards Wiesbaden. Here soon it would link up with Patton's Third Army.

Above left: The pontoon bridge takes shape. *Below:* Assault crossing at St Goar. *Below right:* A Ninth Army convoy of trucks and jeeps makes towards Munster

Not without reason, the Supreme Commander who had watched the original crossing and confessed to a somewhat scared young private waiting to get into his assault boat that he was nervous too, knew now that these successful crossings of the Rhine meant the end of Nazi Germany. As he wrote later in his own account of the campaign: 'The 24th March Operation sealed the fate of Germany. Already, of course, we had secured two bridgeheads further to the south. But in each of these cases, surprise and good fortune had favored us. The northern operation was made in the teeth of the greatest resistance the enemy could provide anywhere along the long river. Moreover, it was launched directly on the edge of the Ruhr and the successful landing on the eastern bank placed strong forces in a position to deny the enemy use of significant portions of that great industrial area.'

Thus it was with four Allied armies across the last major water barrier, the question now arose of what was to be the next move, and, in particular, what was to be the fate of the enemy's greatest industrial area, the Ruhr, for over a century the heart of Germany's industrial potential.

The
Ruhr
plan

In September 1944, some six months before the Rhine was actually crossed, General Eisenhower, the Supreme Commander, had written: 'We shall soon, I hope . . . be in possession of the Ruhr, the Saar and the Frankfurt area . . . Clearly Berlin is the main prize. There is no doubt whatsoever, in my mind, that we should concentrate all our energies and resources on a rapid thrust to Berlin . . . Simply stated, it is my desire to move on Berlin by the most direct and expeditious route.'

That September the official plan had called for a major drive to be made by Field-Marshal Montgomery in the north. Reinforced by as many US divisions from 12th Army Group as Bradley could spare, Montgomery's 21st Army Group would 'leap the Rhine, cap the Ruhr and force a corridor to Berlin', to use General Bradley's description of the Montgomery attack. However, this major thrust to the north would of necessity limit most of the activities of Bradley's 12th Army Group and give the American army a subsidiary role, with most of its commanders naturally gaining little of the glory entailed in this final grand single thrust to the enemy capital.

But Eisenhower had had no opportunity to put his September plan into operation. First his armies had been bogged down by their lack of supplies, and just when that problem had been overcome, the Germans had launched their major counter-offensive in the Ardennes, putting an end to any hope of crossing the Rhine in 1944.

The Battle of the Bulge had ended with a serious breakdown of relationships between the American Bradley and the Englishman Montgomery. The former felt that his own reputation and that of the United States Army had been severely damaged by

Eisenhower's plan is foiled by the Ardennes Offensive, which succeeded in delaying the end of the war

the fact that a foreigner, Montgomery, had been given command of the major part of the 12th Army Group troops during the decisive phase of the battle. Moreover Montgomery's remarks after the battle, or at least Bradley's interpretation of them, had contributed to deepening the rift between the two senior Allied commanders.

Thus it was that when the discussion again turned to the Allied strategy for the post-Rhine crossing period in the early months of 1945, Bradley was no longer prepared to accept the September solution. Although we do not know the precise details of how Bradley approached Eisenhower during the months of February and March 1945, it is clear from Bradley's own remarks and those of staff officers close to him that he presented his case for a revised post-Rhine strategy from a narrow personal and nationalistic point. As he repeatedly told

visitors from SHAEF and presumably Eisenhower himself during their private discussions, 'the prestige of the United States Army is at stake'.

In particular, he wanted the advance into Germany to continue on a broad front 'in depth to guard the rear areas against counterattack and sabotage' as he described his motives for the suggestion, with a double enveloping movement around the Ruhr by two US armies. For him the German industrial area was 'our primary terrain objective'. Then, without the Ruhr, 'Germany would be unable to support its armies in the field'.

As a consequence of this belief that the Ruhr was the major strategic objective because of its economic importance, Bradley suggested: 'To snuff out this industrial furnace, I proposed to Eisenhower that we isolate it with a double envelopment.

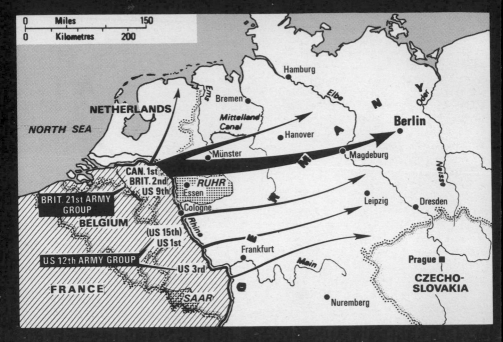

Eisenhower's original plan for the drive into Germany would have by-passed the Ruhr

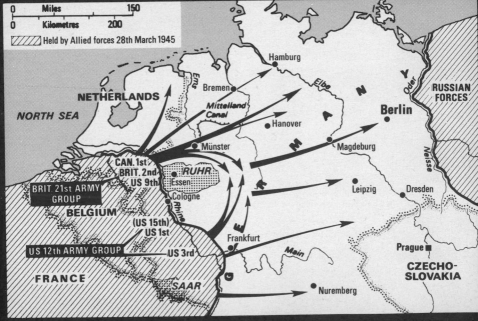

The final plan, laid down in March 1945, called for an encirclement of the Ruhr by the American armies

While Montgomery rimmed the Ruhr from the north across the plains of Westphalia, we would encircle it from the south with our US forces.'

At this juncture one might ask how vital was the Ruhr in the spring of 1945. At the end of February Hitler apparently thought that the great industrial area was highly important to the total German war effort, and he ordered that a barrier between Krefeld and Wesel must be held 'at all costs' so that coal and steel could be transported from the Ruhr by means of the Dortmund-Ems and Mittelland Canals. Yet twenty days later on 19th March, i.e. before the Allies had crossed the Rhine, he commanded that all factories and means of transport within the Ruhr must be destroyed and the general 'scorched earth' policy be implemented.

For the Allies, of course, the Ruhr had always symbolised Germany's major source of military potential. Air Marshal Harris had made it the key to his area bombing in his (mistaken) belief that if he could knock out the centres of industrial production with his bombers, he would contribute decisively to the shortening of the war. As a result the Ruhr had been bombed persistently from the earliest days of the bomber offensive, the raids getting progressively heavier as the years went by.

Yet what many of the Allied planners, obsessed by this vision of the Ruhr as one gigantic military workshop supplying the weapons for the German conquest of the world, seemed to overlook was that the Ruhr only produced steel plating and heavy artillery. Throughout the war it did not manufacture one single aeroplane, for instance, and even at the peak of its production in September 1944, it was only turning out one-tenth of Germany's tanks. Even the French, who had been possessed by a particularly strong phobia about the Ruhr ever since the time of the Franco-Prussian war and were inclined to be very subjective about the area, had to concede that the Ruhr contributed, at the most, a mere twenty-five per cent of the German total war production.

Even so the Ruhr was naturally a vital industrial area. But by the spring of 1945, the years of Allied raids were finally beginning to have their effect. After the raids of early March 1945, industrial production in towns such as Duisburg and Essen was stopped completely for days at a time. Everywhere the population began to leave the grey battered industrial towns in their thousands and even if these people had been prepared to stick by their machines in their shattered factories, the resultant weapons of war would have had to remain in the Ruhr. As we shall see the Allies had virtually severed the Ruhr from the rest of Germany in February-March 1945 by the strategic bombing of the railways and canals leaving the area.

By that spring, according to a US investigation team which surveyed the situation on the spot immediately after the war, the Allied bombings of early 1945 had reduced coal production by only three per cent. But production of vitally needed steel had fallen by between 25 and 30 per cent. Yet in spite of the rapidly decreasing importance of the Ruhr as an industrial centre, Bradley was to have his way; the Ruhr would be objective number one in April.

On 28th March, when Montgomery's 21st Army Group broke out of its Rhine bridgehead, the British commander still believed that his objective was to drive hard from his present positions to the River Elbe. To his right would be the US Ninth Army, with its thirteen divisions under his command and its primary objective Magdeburg, though it would also assist the 12th US Army Group's First Army troops coming up from Remagen in their 'mopping-up' of the Ruhr. Great stress was to be laid on the armoured formations going all

out and avoiding being delayed by local actions.

But on the evening of that day Montgomery received a letter from Eisenhower, which changed the British commander's plans utterly. It read in part: 'I agree generally with your plan up to the point of gaining contact with Bradley to the east of the Ruhr. But thereafter, my present plans . . . are outlined in the following paras.

'As soon as you and Bradley have joined hands in the Kassel-Paderborn area, Ninth Army will revert to Bradley's command. He will then be responsible for occupying and mopping up the Ruhr . . .

'Your Army Group will protect Bradley's northern flank with the inter-army group boundary similar to Second Army's right boundary, Münster-Hannover inclusive to Bradley.'

When Montgomery asked Eisenhower to reconsider this decision, which had burst like a bombshell at his headquarters, the latter replied: 'Bradley must bring the situation in the Ruhr under control before he can initiate the thrust to Leipzig. Certain forces of the Ninth and First Armies must

be employed to achieve this quickly. These must be reinforced and relieved speedily by divisions of the Fifteenth Army using the Rhine bridges of the Ninth and First Armies. Clearly one commander should control a mopping up task of this nature, in such a densely populated area. Furthermore, it is Bradley who will be straining to unleash his thrust to the east and it is very desirable that he should be in a position to judge when the Ruhr situation warrants it.'

Whatever personal, and not mainly military, considerations were behind the changed Allied strategy, and I think today that students of the war increasingly realise that personalities and prestige played an important role in this strange and unexpected *volte face* by Eisenhower on 28th March, it meant that Montgomery's forces would be limited to little more than a flanking operation for the rest of the war. The Ruhr would now occupy the attentions of nearly half Bradley's troops (the First, Ninth, and Fifteenth Armies), while the 'glittering prize' of the German capital was left to the Russians.

For the next two weeks, the Ruhr area was to occupy the major atten-

The bombing of the Ruhr; *Left:* The dock area of Düsseldorf still burns the day after the raid. *Above:* The ruins of Cologne. *Below:* Duren after bombing

The Krupps armament complex at Essen after Allied bombing. Industrial capacity
was impaired

Left above: The devastated Limburg marshalling yards. *Left:* A B-17 pounds air bases. *Above:* Shermans continue the advance. *Right:* Troops are wary of snipers

tion of the three northern US armies; as Eisenhower put it himself 'Bradley's advance with his three armies was to begin as soon as he had made sure that the German forces in the Ruhr could not interfere with his communications.' Although Eisenhower had no intention of conducting a bitter, house-to-house battle for the destruction of the Ruhr garrison, which would fall of its own accord because of hunger and spare the Allies great numbers of casualties, his decision did envelop some twenty-six American divisions in much unnecessary fighting and a time-wasting battle for ground. At this time, except for the defensive line of the River Elbe, there was little to stop the Allies, with their overwhelming strength, from going straight for Berlin, the capture of which by the West might have changed the whole course of post-war Central European history.

Model reacts

The industrial importance of the Ruhr had been greatly reduced by the time the Allies were preparing to surround it in March, 1945. It had been hammered for years by British and later American bombers, and the Allied air forces had launched a full scale interdiction assault in February of that year to cut all communications leading out of the Ruhr eastwards. As part of Operation Clarion, a single day operation on 22nd February, all the Allied air forces struck the Ruhr a heavy blow, leaving only eight of the seventeen key railway centres active. Two weeks later Bomber Command launched its heaviest attack of the war on the Ruhr. On 11th March 1,000 aircraft dropped 4,662 tons on Essen. A day later 1,100 aircraft dropped 4,800 tons on Dortmund. In addition, the RAF and USAF began a systematic sealing-off of the Ruhr from the rest of Germany in February, destroying bridges and viaducts on the general line Bremen-Marburg-Koblenz. On 14th March the Bielefeld viaduct carrying the Hanover-Hamm railway was destroyed by an RAF ten-ton bomb and the Ruhr was finally cut off by the 24th.

Nevertheless there were still very strong German forces located in the area, at least numerically. Although sealed off, they were in a formidable defensive position. To the north, the flanks of the Ruhr troops were protected by the Dortmund-Ems Canal and in the south by the River Sieg. The latter was a difficult undertaking for an attacking force, however superior. Then even if the enemy succeeded in getting across, he would find himself in a dense industrial area which offered the skilled commander manifold possibilities for surprise counter-attacks and stubborn defensive actions. In short, the industrial Ruhr could be an attacking commander's nightmare, for each of many interlocking grimy coal-and-steel cities was capable of swallowing whole

Extension of the Ruhr bombings: Dortmund receives harsh treatment in the effort to isolate the Ruhr

Field-Marshal Kesselring

divisions of infantry in battles where the Allied superiority in air and armour would count for very little. As Field-Marshal Kesselring, the new German Commander-in-Chief in the West, explained: 'The Ruhr was an enigma for any assailant, its capacity for resistance being utterly incalculable . . . The Ruhr provided its own protection.'

But in this densely populated area, the defence depended to a certain extent on the morale of the remaining civilian population, especially as once the communications to the rest of Germany were cut, the military would depend upon the civilians for support and supplies. But the morale of the Ruhr, notoriously left-wing in politics by tradition and cowed by the years of heavy bombing, was not good. In the big cities up to three quarters of the housing had been destroyed and as individual cooking was no longer possible, many were fed by travelling kitchens as in London in the worst days of the 'Blitz'. The able-bodied men were either in the pits or at the front. Their work in the factories was carried out by their womenfolk, who spent their days at the mercy of the Allied bombers or fighters which roared with impunity over the

countryside at tree-top level, and their nights in the cellars below the rubble. It soon became evident, when the Americans started to enter the area, that the civilians could not be relied upon. Taking power into their own hands, they surrendered their towns and villages to the invader whether the military liked it or not. The morale of Army Group B at that time is a debatable subject. In his comments upon the men under his command, Kesselring states: 'The enormously costly battles of the last half year and constant retreat and defeat had reduced officers and men to a dangerous state of exhaustion. Many officers were nervous wrecks, others affected in health, others simply incompetent, while there was a dangerous shortage of junior officers. In the ranks, strengths were unsatisfactory, replacements arriving at the front insufficiently trained, with no combat experience, in driblets and, anyway, too late. They were accordingly no asset in action. Only where an intelligent commander had a full complement of experienced subalterns and a fair nucleus of older men did units hold together.'

But in spite of this rather harsh comment on the quality of his men by a commander who should know, there were units of Army Group B which were prepared to fight and fight hard as the actions of the SS Battle Group *Westfalen* at Paderborn and the assorted Wehrmacht units at Dortmund Air Field were soon to show. Yet, on the whole, Kesselring's assessment of the fighting quality of the men of Army Group B was correct. The men of the two armies, the Fifth Panzer and the Fifteenth, were basically prepared to fight only as long as their officers made them and as long as they felt they had some prospect of winning. After that they were prepared to surrender or desert.

Perhaps somehow the strange and still unexplained apathy of their commander Field-Marshal Model in that last month of his life may have

Above: Civilians help themselves to food when and where they can. *Below:* The flood of civilian surrenders begins

affected their will to resist. For that April after six years of war, which had taken him from one glittering success to another, even in the bad years, Model seemed to have finally lost his nerve and sunk into a dangerous state of subjective indecision.

Walter Model was a representative of the newer type of Wehrmacht officer, who had begun to appear in the late thirties and take their place in the higher ranks of the German army side by side with the older scions of the Prussian aristocracy. Like Rommel, Model had made a name for himself at the beginning of the war as a dashing leader of armoured formations. Later in Russia he had built up a reputation for himself as a ruthless hard-driving advocate of the offensive, which reached its peak when German tank armies met their Waterloo at Kursk in Russia in 1943.

After that Model proved himself as skilled in defence as he had been in attack in the early, more successful years of the war. In Russia, Holland (at Arnhem) and in France, he had demonstrated his flair for improvisation and defence under adverse conditions. As a result the undersized, somewhat gross looking yet exceedingly energetic field-marshal, who affected a monocle in the older Prussian tradition, was respected not only by the regular army but also by Hitler, who as a rule had a poor opinion of the products of the German general staff, of which Model was one. Thus it was that Model, the forceful leader who was characterised by his brilliant operations officer 31-year-old Colonel Günther Reichhelm with the Goethe quotation *'Den lieb' ich, der Unmögliches begehrt'* (I love him who craves the impossible), gained Hitler's confidence increasingly in the last two years of the war. Because of this, Model was given a much freer hand than most of his contemporaries so that he was able to demonstrate his skill as a field commander more easily than his fellow army commanders.

Time and time again in previous months Model had succeeded in restoring seemingly hopeless situations, such as after the almost complete collapse of the German army in Russia in the summer of 1944 and in the West after the disaster of France. But in the spring of 1945 the little field-marshal seemed to one senior German officer who was close to him at that time as if he were 'wrestling with himself to find a solution to some inner conflict. Like all senior commanders he was faced with an insoluble dilemma; as a highly qualified officer he saw the hopelessness of further resistance, but on the other hand, he was bound in duty and honour to his superiors and subordinates.'

But Model was not so utterly loyal to Hitler and the Nazi creed not to realise that if he carried out the Führer's 'scorched earth' policy to burn every factory and destroy every mine abandoned by his men it would mean the complete economic ruin of central Germany in the decade to follow the end of the war. Secretly he agreed to follow Speer's suggestions, which were to sabotage Hitler's intentions wherever possible.

Yet he also knew that if he surrendered to the Allies, his own personal fate would be at stake, as he was on the list of German general officers wanted by the Russians as 'war criminals'. If he did not surrender, then he risked the lives of thousands of innocent civilians. If he did, he risked his honour as a German soldier and perhaps his life at the hands of the Russians. It was a quandary, which fortunately for the Americans, blunted Model's ability to make decisions and carry them out swiftly and forcefully. As Kesselring has summed up his own attitude to Model in that period: 'Model's proverbial energy let me down, however; to this day even, the operations of Army Group B remain incomprehensible to me.'

But now with the Allied attack about to burst upon him, the strangely

Above: Entering the ruins of the devasted town of Altenkirchen. *Below:* 9th Armored Division moves through still smoking Bendorf

Third Army infantry advance rapidly through Kassel

apathetic Model had to do something. He assumed that the main Allied thrust would come from Montgomery and be towards the north, although Kesselring warned him repeatedly of the danger of the imminent threat presented by Hodges' bridgehead around Remagen. Model ignored the warning and moved his headquarters to the extreme right wing of the Ruhr to the small town of Olpe. This decision soon resulted in a break with his commanders in the centre and the left wing, and according to Kesselring had a decisive effect on the coming battle. As the Commander-in-Chief saw it, the move to Olpe meant that Model cut himself off from the correct objective approach to the battle. He became too involved and helped to create the disastrous Ruhr Fortress idea, which would never have arisen if he had placed himself behind the centre of his Army Group. Here, according to Kesselring, Model 'would have gathered in the divisions from the Ruhr and with them have created the frame for a cohesive front farther in the rear. At any rate the central Army Group command would not have been left suspended in the air.'

In spite of Kesselring's protestations, Model continued to organize his defences as he saw fit. He had at his disposal the Fifth Panzer Army, the bulk of Zangen's Fifteenth Army, two corps of Army Group H's First Parachute Army, seven corps of nineteen divisions, plus an estimated 100,000 anti-aircraftmen and their flak cannon, which were thickly sown over the vital industrial area. After the capitulation of the Ruhr, it was estimated that Model started the battle with approximately 320,000 men. But how to use these men? In the first days after the Allied crossing of the Rhine at Remagen and Wesel, a strong full-scale counter-attack might have done the trick. But Model failed to launch it. Later when the Allied bridgeheads across the Rhine had become too formidable for such a counterattack and the Allied commanders had begun to send out probing armoured columns, a series of limited counterattacks aimed at blocking the roads behind the armour and wiping out the tanks in isolation might have succeeded. But again Model failed to move. When Kesselring, who made both these suggestions to Model, saw him at his battle HQ on 26th March, Model agreed with his Commander-in-Chief, but took no action, indicating that it was too late to rally his men and things had gone too far anyway.

Thus it was that when Hodges' First Army broke out of its Remagen bridgehead for the decisive push north on 25th March, it made astonishing progress. Together with Patton's Third Army to its right flank, it created a great bridgehead ninety miles wide from the Sieg river in the north to the Main in the south, then drove up the Lahn valley to Kassel. There Hodges' men formed the southern arm of the pincers to envelop the Ruhr, the other being Simpson's Ninth Army coming from the north.

Three powerful corps led the drive. In two days the Americans drove forty-five miles east of the Rhine against weak and scattered resistance. They crossed the River Dill crushing a German corps and separating Zangen from his Fifteenth Army, leaving him with a handful of HQ personnel and his staff. Roaming the enemy rear areas at will, the swift moving American columns seemed complete victors of all they surveyed. Resistance was minimal. A roadblock covered by a spandau machine gun, an occasional last ditch fanatic or group of youths armed with a *panzerfaust*, a lone panzer lurking in the trees. That was all. While the III, V and VII Corps drove twenty miles on, seizing Marburg and Giessen on the upper Lahn, Patton's XII Corps broke out of the Third Army's Oppenheim bridgehead, swept to Hanau and Aschaffenburg on the Main before charging on at a mad pace to Giessen,

Above: Aschaffenberg still resists; the bombing continues. *Right:* Major-General Maurice Rose (centre)

some thirty miles forward, there to link up with First Army elements.

Leading Hodges' drive forward was the 3rd Armored Division, commanded by General Rose, of V Corps, with Task Force Richardson up in front. Late on the night of 28th March, Lieutenant-Colonel Richardson was ordered to report to Colonel Howze, commander of the Division's Combat Command Reserve. Here he was joined by his comrade Colonel Sam Hogan. Quickly Howze briefed them on their new assignment. He pointed to the small town of Paderborn on the map, some 100 miles to the north northeast, and told them they had to take it.

Richardson could not believe his eyes. 'You mean get to Paderborn in one day?' he exclaimed.

Howze explained. 'Tomorrow morning you leave for Paderborn. Just go like hell. Get the high ground at Paderborn airport.' With Richardson

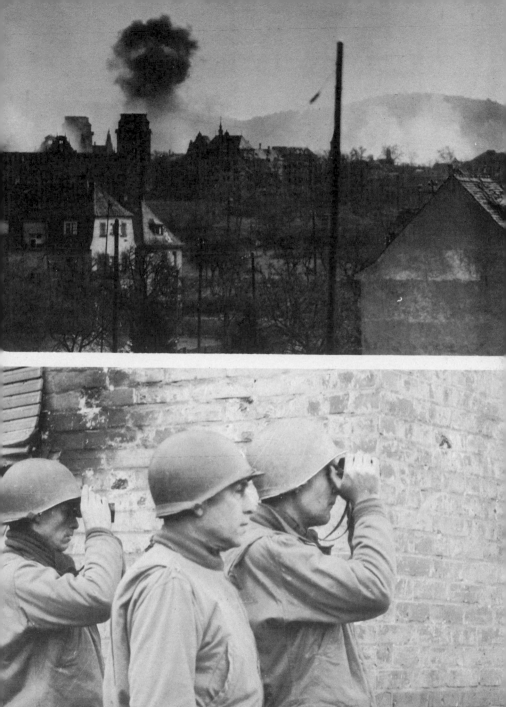

Signal Corps cameraman records the wreckage of a German truck destroyed by 3rd Armored Division, First US Army

would be Hogan, slightly echeloned to the left, and Task Force Welborn from another combat command to his right. The rest of the 3rd Division would follow as best it could. The order was to get to Paderborn without stopping, where the Division would link up with Ninth Army's 2nd Division which had already started its breakthrough to the north of the Ruhr.

At 6 am on the morning of 29th March 1945 Task Force Richardson set off at full speed, a mobile experienced aggressive column, with tanks and half tracks in the lead, and trucks filled with infantry following. All morning they raced north without trouble. At noon they destroyed a passenger train. Once they came to a roadblock, but Richardson simply charged through it with his tanks. By dusk the force had covered seventy-five miles with neglible op-

position, but fog was beginning to roll in.

Richardson pushed on. Some time later he received a message from the divisional commander to clear the small spa town of Brilon. Sending off the main body to do that, he personally sought the best route to Paderborn. A civilian gave him the information he needed but by that time the night was so foggy that he had to get out of his jeep and lead the column on foot. He was in imminent danger of being run over by the tanks behind him, the drivers of which had found a large champagne warehouse in Brilon and were blind drunk by this time.

Thus the advance proceeded towards Paderborn. By midnight Task Force Richardson had covered 109 speedometer miles, and its only casualties were hangovers!

But if the advance of Task Force Richardson was a joke to some people, it was not to the enemy. Model, seeing that he might soon be cut off by the twin pincers edging in on both sides of him, pleaded with Kesselring to let him withdraw his men from the Ruhr while there was still time and at the same time drew up a teletype estimate of the whole situation for the Commander-in-Chief in the West. In it he pointed out that he had failed to contain the enemy at Remagen and prevent the widespread advance across the Rhine. Further continuation of his defence in his existing position, was 'absurd, as such a defence could not even pin down enemy forces.' However Model was willing to go on the offensive. Zangen had just reported to his headquarters bringing news of the advance of the US 3rd Division. The German commander, cut off from his troops, had hidden in a wood with some 200 vehicles until the last of one of Rose's columns had rumbled past. Then using the same dim taillights as the Americans he had joined their column. Sandwiched in between them and a further group of enemy, he had stayed in their line for several hair-raising hours until Brilon where he had turned off on a country road and made his way to a surprised Model, who only could exclaim in surprise, 'You're here?'

Now Model wanted permission to attack eastwards with the LIII Infantry Corps, from a point roughly forty miles west of Paderborn. With this unit he hoped to cut right through the American spearhead and isolate it from the rear. In the meanwhile the American force would soon come up against the dug-in positions of the SS training cadres stationed at the Wehrmacht tank training ground of Paderborn.

The idea looked good to Kesselring especially as it seemed to indicate that Model, a general whom he had long respected, was finally beginning to act positively instead of simply reacting.

Immediately he radioed his approval of Model's decision to attack. But he vetoed the latter's request for permission to withdraw from the Ruhr with the rest of his men without delay in spite of the fact that he, Kesselring,

knew that Model's argument that Army Group B would be urgently needed for the more important battle in central Germany was valid.

Model was quick to point out that he would soon be surrounded and with the resources at his disposal (a corps headquarters, two battle groups and a partially rebuilt infantry division) he could not throw in any significant reserves at any one point so that his army group was eventually doomed to annihilation. But Kesselring refused to approve the breakout.

He did, however, forward the suggestion to the Führer's own headquarters, consoling Model in the meantime with the information that he would assemble a striking force that could break through the Allied held Kassel to the east of the Ruhr and strike into Army Group B, which was soon to be surrounded.

The force Kesselring proposed to use was the 80,000 strong Eleventh Army, under the command of General Lucht, who had gained a good reputation in the initial stages of the Ardennes breakthrough as a corps commander. Lucht's Eleventh Army had been badly hit in the winter fighting in east Prussia when it had lost most of its transport and armoured vehicles to the Russians, but now it was being reconstituted in strong positions in the rugged hills of the Harz, northeast of the Ruhr. If Army Group B could hold out two weeks, which was the period Model had estimated his men could survive an all out American attack, then Kesselring would relieve him with the Eleventh Army. But at all events Model must hold out; the fight for the Ruhr was vital to the Reich. Grimly, knowing that his own death warrant had been virtually signed, Field-Marshal Walter Model gave his orders to the commander of the LIII Infantry Corps, entrenched in the hills of the Sauerland facing General Collins' US VII Corps, to begin his counter attack on the morning of the following day.

Counterattack

While Richardson's men of the 3rd Armored Division slept some six miles outside of Paderborn and the Germans of Army Group B prepared for the battle of the morning, the flying columns of General Simpson's Ninth Army were hurrying to meet them from the other flank of Model's beleagured forces. In the lead was General White's 'Hell on Wheels' 2nd Armored Division. A regular army division, the Second was one of the largest formations on the western front. With its tanks, SPs, armoured cars, half-tracks, trucks, looted German vehicles (even bulldozers), it formed a column more than seventy-two miles long. In order to make a more effective fighting formation out of his unit, fiery cavalryman General White had broken it into the normal three combat commands, but moving in tandem with one held in reserve. Even so the division took nearly twelve hours to pass a given spot.

But in spite of the length of its column and enormous number of its vehicles, the division, which moved at a pace of two miles an hour, was running ahead of virtually every unit of the Ninth Army and had been doing so ever since it had been ordered out of the Rhine bridgehead to link up with the First Army. As befitted a division which had once been trained by the redoubtable General 'Blood and Guts' Patton himself, it moved swiftly to disrupt all communications out of the vital Ruhr valley railway centre of Hamm, then sliced across the autobahn to sever the main supply routes between Berlin and the Ruhr.

Now the Division had covered some fifty miles in three days, by-passing major centres of German resistance, only stopping to fight where there was no alternative route free. Here the Germans usually fought hard, but General White was finding he was being held up more by roadblocks, mined roads and unfavourable terrain than the enemy. In the lead was the 82nd Reconnaissance Battalion,

Above: Army gun crews dig in under fire to defend newly taken autobahn
Below: Distressed civilians loot a stranded train

commanded by Lieutenant-Colonel Wheeler Merriam. Its job was to find the easiest route for the rest of the Division, but Merriam found it a difficult assignment, not because of enemy resistance but because of the utter confusion which seemed to reign everywhere in the German camp.

On 28th March with his light tanks spread out along a railway line running from east to west, Merriam halted to report his new position, suddenly he heard a train whistle and a German troop train heavily laden with armoured vehicles and troops swept by right in front of the guns of the completely surprised tankers. Merriam who was flabbergasted was so close that he could note 'the individual hairs on men's faces where they hadn't shaved'. As the train headed west, Merriam stared at it and then at his men in complete disbelief. Not a shot had been fired on either side!

But that oversight was soon remedied. Merriam shook himself out of his daze and grabbed the radio telephone. A few miles to the west, commanding General I D White saw the train at the same time that he heard Merriam's voice shouting a warning over the phone. But the general too failed to act promptly, While he stood there almost mesmerised, an MP directing his troops across the railway lines, raised his hand and stopped the flow of vehicles – and let the German train roll by!

Then White pulled himself together. He snapped a radio order to the 92nd Field Artillery. A few minutes later they opened fire and sliced the train cleanly in two. The German troop train came to a sudden and very surprised halt, for the German occupants too had not anticipated seeing the Americans so far forward. They had thought the enemy was still on the Rhine. As surprised as their new captors they went off to the POW cage, leaving behind on the train rich booty, including numerous anti-tank guns, field pieces and an enormous

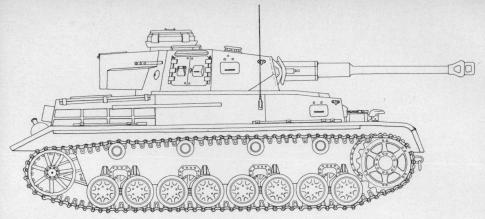

The PzKw IV, the backbone of the German Panzer forces through most of the war, was first produced in 1936, and was quickly modified in the light of operational experience, particularly as regards the improving of armor protection and the increase in gun power. The PzKw IV F2 was the first of the model to mount a long barrelled 75mm gun. *Crew*: 5. *Weight*: 25 tons. *Armament*: one 75mm KwK 40/43 with 87 rounds and two 7.92mm machine guns with 3,150 rounds. *Speed*: 25mph (road) and 10mph (cross country). *Armour*: 85mm front, 30mm side, 11mm top and 20mm rear

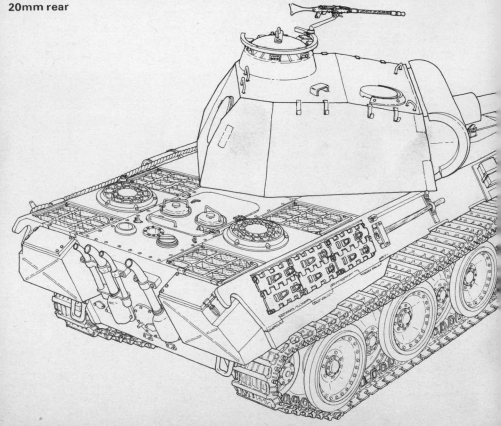

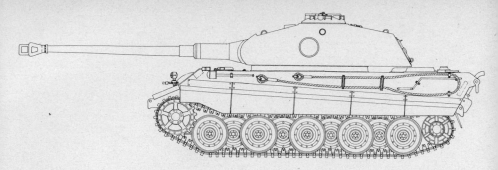

The PzKw VI Tiger II was the German army's heaviest tank of the Second World War. It was very heavily armoured (the armour was also very well angled and shaped) and was gunned with the powerful long-barrelled 88mm gun. Though the Tiger II was underpowered, and therefore lacked manoeuvrability, and unreliable, it proved itself to be an excellent defensive weapon – which was what the Germans needed at the end of the war. The type was first met by the Allies in August 1944 in Normandy. *Crew:* Five. *Weight:* 67 tons. *Armament:* one 88mm gun and two 7.29mm machine guns. *Ammunition:* 78 rounds of 88mm and 5,850 rounds of 7.92mm *Armour:* 100mm lower front and turret front, 150mm upper front, 80mm sides and 40mm top surfaces. *Speed:* 25mph on roads, 13mph cross country. *Range:* 106 miles maximum. The model illustrated here is fitted with a Porsche turret

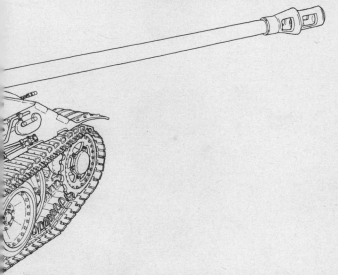

The Panther was perhaps Germany's best tank of the war, and was influenced, as far as design went, by the superlative Russian T-34. This is especially true of the low silhouette and the good sloping of the armour. The Panther was pushed into production very quickly, and therefore suffered from a large crop of teething troubles to begin with, but once these had been sorted out, the tank was more than a match for Allied vehicles. *Crew:* 5. *Weight:* 45.5 tons. *Speed:* 28 mph (road) and 15.5 mph (cross country). *Length overall:* 29 feet 0¾ inches. *Width:* 10 feet 8¾ inches. *Height:* 9 feet 10 inches. *Armament:* one 75-mm gun with 82 rounds and up to three 7.92mm machine guns with 4,200 rounds. *Armour:* 80mm (front), 110mm (turret front), 40mm (side), 15mm (top) and 40mm (rear)

Left: Major-General Joseph L Collins. *Above:* Infantry advance to take an enemy held position

sixteen-inch railway gun.

The advance of the 2nd Armored continued. The lead battalions began to run out of maps. In the case of the resourceful 82nd Reconnaissance Battalion, its forward platoons helped themselves to find their way with the silken emergency escape maps usually issued to Allied pilots in case they were shot down over German territory. Others were equally resourceful, including Lieutenant Arthur Hadley, a pyschological warfare expert attached to the 2nd Division, who found his way by means of the maps in a tattered ancient Baedeker tourist guide. Some were less fortunate or resourceful. One battalion found it had only two maps in the whole unit to show the area of its proposed advance.

But in spite of the Germans, the confusion, and the lack of information, the 2nd Armored Division pressed home its advance. General White saw the drive to the Elbe as his main objective and was not over concerned

with the proposed link-up with the First Army. The determined wiry commander of the 'Hell on Wheels' division had his eyes on Berlin. Already before the division's crossing of the Rhine, Isaac White had ordered his operations officer, Colonel Briard Johnson, to draw up a line of advance to Berlin and by 25th March detailed orders and map overlays were ready.

But White was not fated to get to Berlin, at least not during the war. Already a dangerous situation was beginning to develop on the First Army's front which would require his assistance and consequently delay his drive to the River Elbe and the glittering prize which he thought lay beyond for his division.

Just outside Paderborn Lieutenant-Colonel Richardson of the 3rd Division was ready to move off, unaware that some forty miles to his rear, a German force was about to do the same, its aim being to cut him off from his base. At dawn Richardson started his

Brigadier-General James E Moore

attack on Paderborn. At a crossroads the first two of his leading tanks were hit and knocked out by a lone German Panther. Two miles further on at a small hamlet some three miles from the old Catholic town of Paderborn, long time residence of bishops and the medieval Hansa merchants, a sizeable force of Panthers and Tigers attacked suddenly. A savage bitter little fight developed. In the end both sides withdrew several hundred yards to lick their wounds and decide what to do next.

Richardson came to the conclusion that the Germans were too strong for him. He needed air support. He radioed back to division for fighter bombers. But he was told that the heavy clouds made air support at that low level impossible. Short of fan belts, fuel and ammunition, Richardson called again and asked for an air drop of these urgently needed supplies. 'No aircraft available' came back the laconic answer. A few moments later Richardson was called back to the radio telephone to receive even worse news. The Germans had counterattacked to the division's rear. Task Force Richardson was cut off. The task force commander decided that there was nothing he could do except dig in and see what would happen next.

The LIII Corps, to which Model had given the task of breaking off the 3rd Armored spearhead, was commanded by Major-General Fritz Bayerlein, a veteran of Africa and Normandy where he had commanded the elite Panzer Lehr Division. Bayerlein was a highly experienced and tough commander who, unlike so many of his fellow generals whose experience had been gained primarily in the east, knew the Anglo-American way of battle and had a healthy respect for their artillery and air power. In addition, he knew the weakness of his men. Although he included in his corps such experienced formations as the Panzer Lehr and the 3rd Panzer, he realised that the old spirit had gone and that he could only rely upon his men if their objectives were limited and reasonable.

In spite of the poor combat morale of his men and his lack of ammunition and fuel, Bayerlein set about his task with his accustomed dash and vigour, unleashing his corps from the wooded hills of the Sauerland against the Americans now strung out over seventy miles from the Rhine to Paderborn. Collins reacted at once. He rushed the 1st Division's 16th Infantry Regiment to Buren just below Paderborn, with its 1st and 2nd Battalions positioned on Gesehe, where VII Corps Intelligence thought the Germans might break through and threaten the proposed link-up of the First and Ninth Armies. In addition, he ordered the veteran 9th Infantry Division to give support to the 8th Infantry Division which was strung out for many miles to the rear of the rampaging 3rd Armored.

The 8th Infantry Division, which had taken considerable punishment in the battle for Brest in Brittany and many another Third Army battle since, was led by tough General Moore,

Above: Another truck load of German troops swells the ranks of those who have surrendered. *Below:* Resistance is still locally fierce however and the useless destruction continues

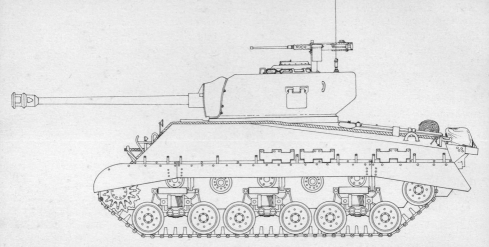

The M4A3 – E8 model of the basic Sherman medium tank was introduced in 1944. *Crew :* Five. *Weight :* 37.1 tons. *Speed :* 26mph on roads. *Radius of action :* 155 miles under optimum conditions and on roads. *Armament :* one 76mm gun with 71 rounds, one .5-inch machine gun with 600 rounds and one .3-inch machine gun with 6,250 rounds. *Armour :* Front 2 inches, sides 1.5 inches, turret front 3 inches, turret sides 2 inches and mantlet 3.5 inches. *Length :* 19.3 feet. *Width :* 9.8 feet. *Height :* 9.9 feet

who although he had known from intelligence sources that the German LIII Corps was going to attack him, threw his men across the River Sieg with the key town of Siegen as their objective. But on that first day of April the Germans fought desperately in spite of their generally poor morale and many of the division's objectives had to be taken and retaken time and time again. At the village of Birken, for instance, the enemy counter-attacked and struck the command post of an anti-tank platoon of the 13th Infantry Regiment located in a farmhouse. The sentry on duty at the time was PFC Walter Wetzel, who warned the men sleeping all around him that the Germans were coming and while the GIs hurriedly groped for their weapons, held off the Germans single-handed. In spite of his rapid rifle fire, several German soldiers reached the farmhouse and began lobbing grenades through the window. Yelling a warning, Wetzel flopped on the grenades and was mortally wounded. Given a moment's respite by the young soldier's sacrifice, the men of the anti-tank platoon were able to get to the windows and break up the attack. Wetzel was awarded the Medal of Honor posthumously.

On that day the Germans launched seventeen counterattacks against the Americans and although the Golden Arrow Division (as it was called from its divisional patch) managed to hold them off, it did lose one of its two bridgeheads across the River Sieg when the 12 Volksgrenadier Division hit it in overwhelming strength.

Under these circumstances, General Collins ordered the 9th Infantry Division into action to stop the Germans emerging from their break-out area around Winterberg and Meschede-Brilon, three small towns famous as ski-centres before the war.

At 0115 hours on the morning of 1st April, the 9th Division moved off from the small town of Hallenberg, with its 3rd Battalion to the left and the 1st to the right. The terrain was difficult. High wooded hills were broken up everywhere by fast moving streams, still icy cold although it was already spring. In addition the narrow curving roads were blocked by minefields and barriers virtually everywhere. To make matters worse, visibility in the hills was bad and although the Americans made some progress up the valley leading to the resort town of Winterberg, in which the winter Olympics of 1936 had been held, General Craig, the divisional commander, ordered the advance halted for the day; the risk of progressing further into the hilly area through fog and without air cover was too great, he felt.

That night the Panzer Lehr, the 3rd Panzer and the 176 Infantry Division (elements of all three divisions were later identified among prisoners) struck the 9th Infantry's 1st Battalion in overwhelming strength at the village of Neu Astenberg. So fierce were the attacks that the Americans were forced to withdraw. They dug in around the village of Mollseifen to the east. Meanwhile a furious battle had developed in the resort town of Hoheleye where the Americans fought fanatical SS troopers in the middle of a snow storm, a freak even for that region in April. The fighting developed into a 'battle in prohibition-days gangster style', as the divisional history put in, with SS men trying to escape in fast cars. As they did not know which roads the Americans held out of town, 'they roared up and down the road firing as they went. The infantry headed for a resort hotel and began battling for the lobby while the Nazis shot it out from behind sofas and chairs and from doors and windows.'

While this gangster-style battle was going on, the division's 47th Infantry Regiment was advancing towards the town of Oberkirchen, which Intelligence regarded as one of the key enemy escape routes because its geographical situation allowed it to control the road net

vital to the German communication and supply system. At 0800 hours on the morning of 2nd April, the regiment's 2nd Battalion went into the attack. It cleared the village of Welminghausen to the south-east of Oberkirchen, but only after severe fighting. The battalion pushed on and entered the next village on the road to Oberkirchen, Vewald. Here they were hit by fire from three Mark IVs and several SPs and stopped for a short while. Again the battalion rallied and pushed on to be attacked in the early hours of the following day by a strong German force of several hundred infantry led by five tanks. Three platoons of the 2nd Battalion were overrun almost immediately and the Germans penetrated Vewald. Individual soldiers fought back with bazookas from the white-washed half-timbered houses of the medieval village and succeeded in knocking out three enemy tanks. Still the Germans came on. Hand to hand fighting developed with the battle swaying back and forth down the cobbled village main street. But in the end the Germans gave way and withdrew leaving seventy-eight men captured in American hands.

By dusk on the evening of 2nd April, the American attack on a line between Winterberg and Oberkirchen had bogged down into a hard slog as had that of the 8th Division on Siegen. German resistance had thickened considerably and the VII Corps was going to take another forty-eight hours before it captured the key heights in that sector, which it needed before it could proceed any further.

But at the same time Bayerlein's counterattack, which was not only intended as a means of cutting off the 3rd Armored spearhead but probably also as a way of opening an escape route for the whole of Army Group B in that area, had come to an abrupt halt after making some eight miles of progress into the American left flank. Kesselring explained LIII Corps' lack of success after the war by maintain-

A fallen SS trooper symbolizes the hopeless but desperate resistance which made the struggle for Oberkirchen so fierce

ing that Model had struck at the wrong spot.

'I differed with Field-Marshal Model in the way he tried to stop the rapid advance south of the Ruhr,' he told interrogators. 'In my personal opinion he should have started his attack further to the east, thereby cutting off the relatively weak points of your advance and restoring a north-south line; rather than allowing his flank to be turned as it was. By attacking too far west Model ran into a much thicker column and was unsuccessful. It is the point at which you strike that makes the difference. One battalion striking at the right point can do far more than a division at the wrong point.'

There is no doubt some truth in what Kesselring had to say. Indeed Model made several bad tactical mistakes during the course of the campaign, including the fatal one of supposing the Allied attack would have its *Schwerpunkt* in the north, i.e. on the Ninth Army's front, with a subsidiary drive coming up from Remagen along the right bank of the Rhine to link up with the Ninth somewhere in the region of Duisburg. But it is more than likely that the reason Bayerlein's counterattack failed was because his men were war-weary and he did not have the necessary supplies of fuel and ammunition to give really effective power and élan to the thrust eastwards. At all events it was clear to the German command by the end of that second day of April, that the escape route to the east had been well and truly cut. The American VII Corps was holding firm and more divisions were hurrying north-east all the time. Bayerlein gave up any further attempts at breaking out. Now he prepared for the American attack on his positions which was bound to come soon, and in force.

Link up

Just after nightfall, Colonel Richardson who was still dug in opposite the German force, which unknown to him was recruited from the staff and students of the SS training camp at the large tank training centre just outside Paderborn, received an urgent radio stating that 'Big Six' was coming to inspect the situation and a jeep was to be sent to meet him.

'Big Six' was the commanding general of the 3rd Armored Division, General Maurice Rose, and the last person Richardson wanted at the front at this particular moment. He radioed back that he had no jeep to spare and ended with the veiled warning, in case the Germans were monitoring his radio frequency, 'Don't send Big Six this way!'

At that moment General Rose was some five miles to Richardson's right, with Colonel John Welborn's task force. The latter had just been informed that the four German Tiger tanks he could see to his front had

already been knocked out by the air force. Confidently he started to advance towards them. For a while nothing happened, but just as his leading tanks began to breast a rise, they were hit by fierce and very accurate 88mm fire from the four tanks. It was a trap. The four Tigers had been hit by the air force, but with napalm and not the usual 500lb 'tank busters'. Welborn and his first three tanks managed to scurry for safety at the bottom of the next valley. The rest of the leading tanks were not so fortunate. In a matter of minutes the next seven Shermans were picked off by the skilled efficient gunners of the tank training school.

Although cut off from Welborn, who was about half a mile to the front, General Rose was well aware of what had happened as the blazing tanks were silhouetted on the horizon and he could make out the different sound of the German 88s and the American 75s. He ordered Task Force Doan,

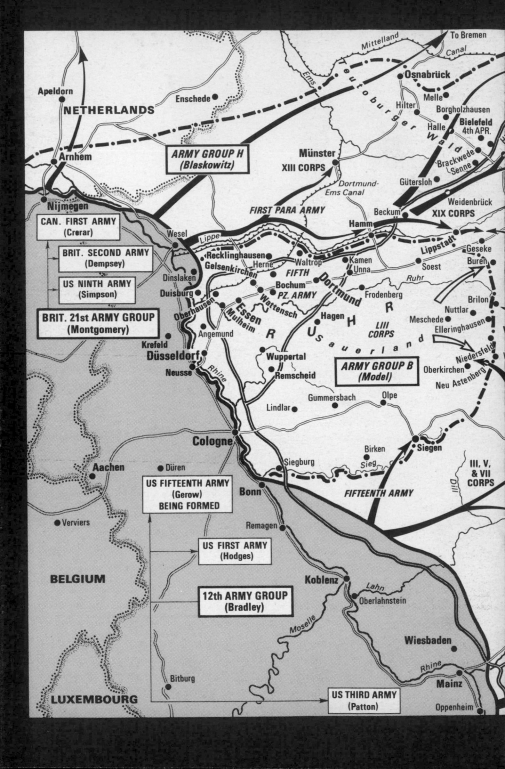

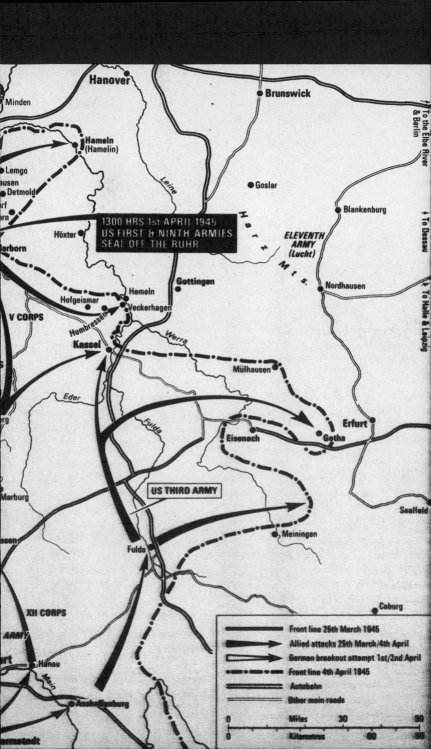

which was coming up to the rear, to render assistance.

But now half a dozen Tigers had appeared to the south-east, forcing their way between Task Force Welborn and Doan. Rapidly this new force knocked out several White half tracks and a tank destroyer. Except for the leading three tanks, which had survived the original German attack, Task Force Welborn and the commanding general of the 3rd Armored Division were well and truly surrounded. German infantry were also visible in position in the woods all around, ready to support their tanks if necessary. In a 'wild scene from Dante's Inferno,' as one officer who was present called it, German tanks came out of the woods to the front of the cut-off column and began to move down the road, machine-gunning men and vehicles. The divisional artillery commander, Colonel Brown, advised Rose to take to the woods, but the latter pointed out that to the front where Welborn had disappeared there was no sound of action. It might be safer to plunge ahead in Welborn's wake.

This the general did with his party of two jeeps, a motor-cyclist and an armoured car. A mile further on from the blazing column, the small group came to a cross-roads. There Rose saw the dim outline of a tank. But it was disabled and as the group approached it, small arms fire broke out on both sides of the road. They retreated to the main road where a big tank came to meet them. For a moment, Rose thought its bulk indicated it was one of the new Pershings allotted recently to his command. But then someone noticed, as the vehicle rumbled by, that it had twin exhausts and not the single one of the Pershing. Quickly the little group reacted.

The first jeep got off the road and escaped. Rose was not so fortunate. The commander of the third German tank spotted the Americans. He poked his head out of the turret and pointed a machine pistol at Rose.

Rose, his driver, and Major Bellinger, his aide, started to unbuckle their weapon belts. Rose, unlike the other two, had his pistol at his waist instead of in the shoulder holster. He reached down to do the job. The German misconstrued the gesture and opened fire. Rose fell to the ground dead.

Later the Ruhr, soon to be surrounded, would be named the 'Rose Pocket' after the dead general, and much later, war crimes teams would investigate the case as a potential war crime because it was known that General Rose was a Jew, the son of a Rabbi, and the troops defending the Paderborn area were mainly from the racially orientated *Waffen SS*. But the investigation proved that the Germans had made a genuine mistake and the charges were dropped.

Now the battle for Paderborn continued. The famous training ground became a battlefield, with the instructors, officer cadets, trainees and members of the demonstration teams putting theory into practice, manning the tanks and anti-tank guns they had so often used before in practice. They fought with vigour and energy stiffened by the example of the ruined city of Paderborn which had been three quarters destroyed in a twenty-seven minute long air raid a couple of days before, it lay completely defenceless without flak. They were determined to hold the ground which was holy to the Wehrmacht and vital to Model who realised that if the Americans took Paderborn they would link up with the US Ninth Army coming up around the north western flank of the Ruhr and he would be trapped.

Brigadier-General Doyle O Hickey, till then commander of Combat Command A, took over the 3rd Division while Colonel Doan replaced him as CCA commander. Together the two men launched an all-out attack on Paderborn, with their main thrust directed now at the airport, which was securely held by a large group of infantry armed with I36 cannon. Angry and vindictive at what they thought

Brigadier-General Doyle O Hickey

was a war crime, the 'murder' of their divisional commander, the men of the 36th Armored Infantry set about their task with a will.

Meanwhile back at the Corps HQ of the VII Corps to which the 3rd Armored belonged General 'Lightning Joe' Collins was worried. But he was worried for the wrong reasons. He still had not learned of Model's counter-attack to the south of 3rd Division which by noon on 31st March had penetrated eight miles into the armoured division's flank, though he had just learned from prisoners that the enemy was to launch a counter-attack against his left flank. Nor did he yet know that Task Forces Richardson and Hogan had been cut off at Paderborn.

He was worried because he felt that the Germans might escape the trap being planned for them. According to the original plan the Ninth Army component of Montgomery's 21st Army Group was to link up with Bradley's 12th Army Group near Paderborn in a few days time. But with the prospect of a German counter-attack looming large, which might delay his own drive forward, he needed more speed on the part of the Ninth

Army to effect the juncture. But he was afraid that Montgomery's slow advance on the northern flank of the Ruhr would mean the failure of the link-up. At that point in the war the great majority of the American senior commanders were critical of Montgomery's caution and lack of drive and the way he used the American troops under his command. They felt that he refused to give the Americans their head and allotted them subsidiary roles in his battles so that the British component of the 21st Army Group would always earn the glory. They also had the somewhat disappointing result of the Falaise Battle in Normandy before their eyes, in which, as they saw it, Montgomery's caution and slowness allowed major German units to escape from the encirclement of the Falaise Pocket, supposed to be the death blow to the German Army in France.

Worried as he was, 'Lightning Joe', who gained his name for his rapid thrusts in the Pacific theatre, took a highly unorthodox step. On the afternoon of 31st March he telephoned his old friend General Simpson, commander of the Ninth Army, and asked for help. Military etiquette frowns upon a corps commander in one army group asking the commander of another group to assist him, but as the news began to flood in of the increased German activity in the 3rd division sector, Collins no longer felt himself bound by the strictures of military formality.

He told Simpson that Monty was moving too slowly and he felt that unless the link-up was made soon the Germans might 'break out toward Paderborn.' He added 'Bill, I'm worried. I'm spread out so thin.'

Then he asked the tall, completely bald-headed commander of the Ninth if he would release a combat command of the 2nd Armored and order it to drive immediately toward Paderborn. He, in turn, 'would send a combat command over to meet them.'

Simpson agreed and, without con-

Above: Simpson and Montgomery with other US generals. There is American concern that Montgomery's tactics could prevent the link up. *Below:* The white flags begin to appear. Abandoned transport vehicles choke a village street

sulting the 21st Army Group commander, ordered elements of the 2nd Armored Division to turn south east and head towards the embattled Third.

Near the head of the leading 2nd Armored column, was 1st Lieutenant William Dooley, commander of E Company of the 67th Armored Regiment. Receiving his orders to move on the night of the 31st, Dooley had no idea of the importance of his mission, in fact, he did not even know exactly where he was going. All he knew was that he had been ordered to push on as fast as possible for the small medieval city of Lippstadt, some twenty-two miles east of Paderborn.

Resistance was scant but Dooley knew that somewhere a great battle was raging. From the south came the steady rumble of heavy guns which at times was so severe that his tanks shook with the vibration. Edging forward in the darkness after the column had been attacked by lone German gunners, then racing on again through the pitch-black night, Dooley covered fifty miles that night. By dawn on Easter Morning 1945 he was on the road between Beckum and Lippstadt. His objective was almost in sight.

In Lippstadt itself, the German military command hesitated between calling the little town an open city and then a 'fortress', to use the term currently popular among the local Nazi leaders. In the end a compromise was reached. Tank traps were erected at every entrance to town. Made of thick cement pipes, filled with concrete and iron, and guarded by a few soldiers, they were supposed to hold off the Americans, while the remaining bridges were blown. In the meantime the remaining garrison would withdraw northwards, taking with them all the foreign workers and POWs, who as the Germans saw it presented a danger to the local populace once the military garrison had been withdrawn. The prisoners were to be sent through the gap between the Allied lines between

Volksturm trooper who surrendered

Münster and Lippstadt and interned once again. Thus the town was made ready to meet the American invaders.

The morning of Easter dawned bright and warm. Everywhere the peach and cherry were heavy with premature blossom. In the strongly Catholic town a few of the older inhabitants tried to go to church, but they were turned back by the local party members. There was no time for church. The town was preparing itself for its last fight. Everywhere the local Hitler Youth and *Volkssturm* were being mustered to take their places at the barricades.

It was six o'clock; a tired Dooley and his men set about clearing the first houses on the outskirts of the town. The remaining German regular troops were in position in the gardens. They opened fire at once with their rifles and machine guns. A German Mark IV appeared and opened fire at the leading Sherman. Luckily the enemy shell struck the right side of the American's turret and ricocheted off. The German fled. The German infantry began to withdraw. Here and there white flags started to appear. In the town itself

the civilians began to plunder the local barrack's storerooms, with the assistance of the remaining supply personnel who did not want their stock to fall into enemy hands. The 67th Armored men approached the first road block warily, but civilians rushed out and removed the cement pipes so that they could pass on.

By 12.30 the Americans had penetrated well into the town's suburbs. Second Lieutenant Donald Jacobsen was ordered into the town itself. An infantry squad had been cut off in a hospital and needed help. Jacobsen loaded his men on tanks and set off. Everywhere white flags and sheets were hanging from the windows of the medieval half-timbered houses. Jacobsen pushed on. Thirty-five Germans surrendered and were loaded onto the tanks. There seemed little sign of enemy resistance anywhere. Suddenly as Jacobson was almost out of town, he spotted tanks coming from the east. Quickly he gave the order to his men to prepare to fight.

Just as he was about to order 'open fire,' he recognised the leading vehicles as being American M-5s. They were

Above: Freed French POWs. *Right:* The town of Ahlem displays white flags as Ninth Army tanks traverse Adolf Hitler street on the way to Lippstadt

from the 3rd Armored. A short time before a fast moving company of the 36th Armored Infantry, Lieutenant Robert Cook's Company C, had rushed Paderborn's airfield and seized it, with the aid of the rest of the 1st Battalion of the 36th Armored. Now patrols had begun to edge out to look for the 2nd Armored.

The time was 1 o'clock on the 1st April 1945. Although Jacobsen and his men, laughing and joking with the First Army soldiers, did not realise the momentous quality of their link-up with the 3rd Division, they had just sealed the fate of over a quarter of a million men of Model's Army Group B plus another 100,000 of Flak Command. The Germans were trapped. The Ruhr Pocket was achieved. As Jacobsen was to say later of his own lack of concern about this historic moment: 'It's amazing how ignorant the fellows who really fight the war are.'

Enter Kesselring

By 1st April 1945, the Allied situation on the Ruhr was a follows: along the northern edge of the pocket, Simpson had his XIX Corps under Major-General Raymond McLain positioned between Paderborn and Hamm at the north eastern tip of the Ruhr to block any egress of Model's Army Group B. They were attempting to link up with the XIII Corps under the command of Major-General Alvan Gillem Jr north-east to Muenster. The advances of these two corps to Paderborn and Münster had split the First Parachute Army down the middle and forced the enemy formation's right wing to fall back to the heights of the *Teutoburger Wald*, a heavily wooded and easily defended position straddling the autobahn northwards at Bielefeld. In all Simpson had a total of one armoured, five infantry and one airborne divisions committed to the Ruhr operation.

To his south and still mainly on the west bank of the Rhine between Cologne and Remagen were the troops of the newly constituted Fifteenth American Army under the command of Lieutenant-General Gerow, which was intended for occupational duties following the surrender of Germany. Committed to the Ruhr operation Gerow had one infantry and two airborne divisions, which were soon to cross the Rhine at company strength and involve themselves in the fighting.

To the east, Hodges of the First Army had one armoured and seven infantry divisions reserved primarily for the fighting soon to come in the heavily industrialised Ruhr. Altogether eighteen divisions of Bradley's 12th Army Group would soon be involved in the operations that were to take place over the next two weeks.

Trapped in the pocket formed by the link-up of the First and Ninth Armies at Lippstadt were all of the Fifth Panzer Army, the bulk of the Fifteenth Army and two corps of the First Parachute Army of Army Group

US tank moves up past
abandoned German gun

H. The area given to them to defend now was thirty by seventy-five miles, a total of 4,000 square miles.

Within this pocket, which contained more German troops than had been trapped at Stalingrad, Tunisia or France, there were munition, gun and tank plants, plus oil refineries which should have been more than capable of supplying all Model's needs for some time to come. However the industry and transport system of the Ruhr had been so dislocated by the intensive bombing of the last two months, that the ammunition and fuel Model so vitally needed could not be produced. In addition Model's ability to fight was limited by the fact that there were still, in spite of mass evacuations, millions of civilians, mainly older men, women and children, shut in with his troops.

It is not surprising, therefore, that Model, who in spite of his somewhat gross features was a sensitive man in many ways, was tortured by what he should do next. There were several possibilities open to him. As we have already stated he could surrender. But he had already publicly condemned Field-Marshal Paulus for his surrender of the Sixth German Army at Stalingrad in 1943, and in addition his own life seemed forfeited if he were handed over to the Russians.

On the other hand, he could turn the Ruhr into a gigantic Stalingrad, as Hitler wished, in which city after city would be fought for, each individual house being defended stubbornly to the end so that at least twenty Allied divisions would be tied up for a considerable period and the pressure on Berlin relieved. If this were done Hitler, according to his own statement, would deal with the Russians and then launch a counterattack from the east to open a way into the Ruhr and relieve Model.

Surrender or defence were the first two alternatives, and neither of them appealed to the stocky little field-marshal who had got the German army out of many a tight corner in these last two years. He was appalled by the economic ruin and sheer human misery which a stubborn defence would bring upon the inhabitants of the Ruhr, especially if he carried out Hitler's 'scorched earth' policy. General von Mellenthin, who knew him during this crucial period of his life, has written of Model's attitude to the Führer's scorched earth decree as follows: 'Model never digressed from the strict path of military discipline, but as a true servant of Germany, he blunted the edge of senseless commands, and sought to minimize unnecessary destruction. Hitler had ordered a 'scorched earth' policy, and wanted us to wreck every factory and mining plant in the Ruhr, but Model limited himself to purely military demolitions. The Field Marshal was determined to preserve the industrial heart of Germany; no longer did he fight stubbornly for every building, and he disregarded the orders issued by the Führer in a last frenzy of destructive mania.'

As for surrender, Model also discussed this alternative with von Mellenthin, although as we have seen the idea was anathema to him. Von Mellenthin describes the situation as follows: 'Model wondered whether he should initiate negotiations with the enemy, and put this question to me frankly. We both rejected it on military grounds. After all, Field-Marshal Model knew no more about the general situation that the simplest company commander in his army group. His ignorance sprang from "Führer Command No. 1" of 13th January 1940, which laid down that "no officer or authority must know more than is absolutely necessary for the execution of his particular task". Model did not know whether political negotiations were going on and he was fully sensible of the argument that the western armies must keep on fighting to the last in order to protect the rear of our comrades in the east, who were involved in a desperate struggle to cover the escape of millions of German

Above: Onward through Munster. *Below:* Infantry of 17th Airborne Division pick up extra ammunition on their way into Munster

Lieutenant-General Leonard T Gerow

women and children, then fleeing from the Russian hordes.'

The result was that on the first day of April 1945, Walter Model saw two possibilities still open to him. He could try to obtain Hitler's permission to make a fighting withdrawal out of the 'pocket', probably eastwards in the direction of the Harz Mountains, ideally located for protracted defence or to the River Elbe itself, where he knew sizeable German formations existed or were in the process of being constituted. Alternatively he could counterattack in force to east or west and hope to break through the Allied cordon. In this way he might be able to link up with either one of the army groups to his flanks and establish some semblance of a firm defensive line in front of the Elbe once more.

But it was the first possibility which interested Model more, especially as he did not wish to turn the Ruhr into an economic desert by allowing it to become a battlefield. That day he waited desperately for Kesselring's transmission of Hitler's answer to

his, Model's, request made two days before for permission to withdraw from the Ruhr. It came with the impact of a bomb.

Returning to his headquarters that day after an inspection trip, Kesselring was told by his chief-of-staff, Westphal, that a new order had been received from the Führer's HQ. It stated that Model was commanded to defend the Ruhr as a fortress. Army Group B was not to break out!

Kesselring, loyal soldier and unimaginative man though he was, found this hard to believe. He knew how desperate the situation in the Ruhr Pocket really was. Although he did not agree with Model's plans for the defence of the area, he still realised that even if his subordinate had been up to his old form, his food supplies would soon hamstring any offensive or defensive operation he undertook. They were only sufficient for two or three weeks. In addition, although he had little respect for Eisenhower's ability as a strategic planner, he knew the American would not be foolish enough to let himself be held up by the Ruhr. As Kesselring saw it, Eisenhower's objective lay further east; that was his strategic target. Nor did Kesselring underestimate the Allies' capacity for the ruthless, perhaps indiscriminate, bombing of the many civilian and military targets present in the Ruhr. Eisenhower, he reasoned, might simply content himself with letting his all powerful air forces do the job of reducing the Ruhr for him while Model was starved into submission.

Obedient soldier that he was Kesselring passed on the Führer's orders to Model and the leader's comment that the Ruhr had to be defended as a 'fortress' in immediate subordination to and under the direct command of the OKW, the German High Command. We do not know Model's reaction when he received the order; it is not recorded. But Kesselring himself notes in his memoirs: 'I was more than flabbergasted by this decision of the OKW. It upset all our plans. The OKW may have thought a break-out had no longer any prospect of success, and that an encircled Army Group might pin down enough enemy troops to prejudice a strong eastward drive.' But, 'The only hope of pinning down strong investment forces lay in a stubborn and indeed aggressive defence, which, judging by what I had seen, was not on the face of it likely.'

At this stage of the war, Field-Marshal Kesselring was probably the best choice Hitler could have made for the defence in the west. The former Bavarian artillery officer who had transferred to an administrative job in the newly created Luftwaffe in 1933 was living proof of Goethe's maxim '*In der Beschraenkung zeigt sich der Meister*' ('the master proves himself in a period of limitation'). From the moment the Axis campaign in North Africa had come to an end Albert Kesselring had guided the German efforts to forestall the Italians' attempt to sue for peace with the Allies and at the same time fight off the repeated Anglo-American assaults. Hampered by an almost complete lack of intelligence as to Allied intentions, as was now the case in Central Germany, he fought the length of Italy on the defensive, tested by a series of surprise situations. Never once did he lose his head, in spite of the fact he was confronted repeatedly by such examples of Allied initiative as the Anzio and Salerno landings. While foregoing offensive action, he spent his energies holding the line and when it was obvious he could hold no longer, extricating his men to fight again at the next best defensive feature.

Kesselring was used to desperate situations. Whatever victories he had achieved in Italy had been only of a temporary nature. With the initiative permanently on the side of the Allies, he knew that they would always attack again. Further, he was used to defensive fighting. Never once did he

Field-Marshal Walter Model

incline to offensive action, save at Salerno. In short Kesselring was the ideal commander to meet up to the situation developing now in central Germany. He was tough, defensively minded and pliable. Above all he had good nerves, something he was going to need urgently in these coming weeks.

Faced now with the fact that he had to carry out Hitler's command and yet at the same time could not afford the loss of Model's Army Group B, which would mean that the whole of central Germany would be handed over to the enemy and a gap blown in his front between Army Groups H and G that he could never again fill, the Commander-in-Chief West looked for some means of getting Model out of the mess he found himself in. Two possibilities presented themselves.

First of all there was the so-called Eleventh Army, which was the remnants of some nine divisions located in the Harz Mountains. The Eleventh Army had suffered severely in the limited February 1945 counterattack against the Russians in east Prussia and had thereafter been withdrawn to the Harz where the terrain would make up for the lack of its tanks which had been mostly lost in the fight against the Russians. Now this 'Army ' if it could be called that, held a tactically sound position in the mountains from which it might be launched against the Ruhr, there to build a solid line along the River Weser, forty miles east of Paderborn and to the west of the Harz mountains.

This 'holding attack' of the Eleventh Army would be then reinforced by the powerful Twelfth Army, a new formation in process of being created in the Elbe area between Dessau and Wittenberg. Although this formation had never been in action as an army, it was one of the best units left in Germany in the spring of 1945. Under the command of General Wenck, a brilliant, forty-five year old officer who had been Guderian's deputy, it was composed of the cream of the German officer-cadet and NCO schools plus the best young men recruited from the Nazi labour organisation, the *Arbeitsdienst*. The Twelfth Army would have one armoured division, *die Clausewitz-Division*, made up from all the tank training schools left in central Germany; one panzer grenadier division, *Schageter*, formed from officer-cadet schools and the *Arbeitsdienst*; and five infantry divisions, with appropriately patriotic names: *Potsdam, Scharnhorst, Ulrich von Hutten, Friedrich Ludwig Jahn* and *Theodor Koerner*.

But on the 1st April 1945, the Twelfth Army still existed only on paper. Kesselring knew he would have to buy time before he could send it into the attack. It would be the job of Model's northernmost formations and the 80,000 men of the Eleventh Army to buy time until the Twelfth came, as Kesselring put it, 'to the rescue.' Then, 'only with its help could there be a certain assurance that the course of events on the Russian front would not be influenced from the west and

One of the effects of war

the splitting of Germany into two halves be prevented . . . The Twelfth Army thus was the all-important factor in the conduct of operations in the west, whichever way the situation developed it could be employed in the Harz Mountains for any task.'

As a result the Harz Mountains had to be held and a certain area to the immediate front of these mountains to be kept open. As Kesselring saw the situation on that day, the key defensive features in the generally open country to the front of the Harz Mountains, the *Teutoburger Wald*, a range of forested hills between the Rivers Ems and Weser; and the River Weser, formed by the confluence of the Fulda and Werra and flowing into the North Sea, must be held to prevent pressure being exerted on the Harz, the site of his assembly area for the attack westwards.

Pointing out the necessity of reinforcing the Harz garrison and keeping open communications between the Harz and Elbe to the OKW in Berlin, he was told that day that the Potsdam Division would be sent up. In addition the 39th Panzer Corps was being prepared for a counter-stroke at combat group strength with the same aim in mind. Now everything depended upon the line of the *Teutoburger Wald* plus the River Weser being held, thus preventing the enemy flooding into the open country and cutting the Harz off by an enveloping movement as had been done with the Ruhr. Clearly Kesselring saw his mission as keeping that Harz base west of the Elbe free for the operations of the Twelfth Army. Without operational freedom for this base, any attempt to extricate Army Group B from the Ruhr Pocket was doomed to failure. As he expressed the major fear that haunted him that April day in his memoirs many years later, Kesselring knew that 'If the enemy reached the open country on either side of the Harz, the game was up.'

The drive for the Weser

The day the encirclement of the Ruhr was completed the Allied supreme commander gave out new orders to his forces. Bradley's Twelfth Army Group was 'to mop up the ... Ruhr ... launch a thrust with its main axis: Kassel-Leipzig . . seize any opportunity to capture a bridgehead over the River Elbe.'

In accordance with these orders, both the Ninth Army and the First prepared to push forward on a two corps front. The Ninth would advance with one corps on each side of the autobahn, penetrate the *Teutoburger Wald* near Bielefeld and cross the last water barrier before the Elbe, the River Weser, between Minden in the north and Hamelin, of Pied Piper fame, in the south. The First Army, not having the advantage of the autobahn for more rapid movement, would pass through more difficult country, advancing to Hofgeismar and from there to the Weser, where they would cross near the little town of Veckerhagen.

The Ninth Army, commanded by Lieutenant-General Simpson, pushed off in grand style. 'My people were keyed up,' he was to recall later, 'We'd been the first to the Rhine and now we were going to be the first to Berlin. All along we thought of just one thing – capturing Berlin, going through and meeting the Russians on the other side.' South of the autobahn, rivalry between General Macon's 83rd Infantry Division and General White's 2nd Armored Division reached a peak as they vied with each other to see who could advance the more rapidly. Tenaciously pacing the 2nd mile for mile, the infantry division thrust forward in a weird and wonderful collection of captured and looted vehicles, which might easily have been mistaken for a German army column but for the number of US vehicles interspersed among them. But if the 'Rag-Tag Circus', as the 83rd became named at this time, confused Allied air reconnaissance somewhat, it confused the enemy even more so. As the division rushed forward, a German staff car, full of high ranking officers, taking one of the 83rd's columns for a German unit began to weave in and out of the surprised American formation, blowing its horn. Finally the Americans reacted and a burst of machine gun fire brought the Mercedes to a surprised halt. The Germans were taken prisoner in the middle of what they had thought to be one of their own outfits. The Mercedes received a hurried paint job and with a US star slapped on its still wet sides was pressed into service.

Opposition, generally, was light. The Ninth took the towns they passed on the autobahn with little effort. A small show of strength or a light artillery bombardment usually sufficed to bring out the white flags and a surrender delegation, led by the local *Bürgermeister*. Even where the Nazi party bosses or the local military commander attempted a defence, they were thwarted in their efforts by the villagers or townsfolk who would remove the tank traps or barriers before they could be used in action. In this way such towns as Wiedenbruck and Gütersloh, which were directly on the path of the Ninth's advance to Bielefeld and the *Teutoburger Wald*, passed into American hands with hardly a shot being fired.

But now the heights of the *Teutoburger Wald* loomed ahead and the commanders of the 5th and 2nd US Armored Divisions which were leading the dash forward to left and right of the autobahn knew that they might expect tougher opposition than they had met in the last forty-eight hours, especially when they reached the large industrial town of Bielefeld, which guarded the pass cut through the rugged hilly woods by the autobahn at Lämmershagen.

In this area, stretching about thirty miles between the villages of Hilter to the west of Bielefeld and Horn to its south east, the enemy front was commanded by Major-General Becher, who had taken over two weeks before.

Lieutenant-General William H Simpson

At that time he had divided his front into three commands: the western flank under Colonel Hulle; the southern flank under Major-General Goerbig; and the centre section, including Bielefeld, under Colonel Sommer. With the aid of these officers, Becher desperately tried to organise some sort of effective defence line against the Americans who were advancing against him in three main columns, one on the autobahn and one to each side of it. Their destination was the passes which led through the *Teutoburger Wald*.

But Becher's resources were strictly limited. His staff was small and inexperienced and as he possessed no signallers, his orders had to be transmitted either by runner, the civilian telephone exchange, or DRs to the seven-thousand-odd men under his command. These men were expected to hold a front normally requiring eight or nine divisions, i.e. 100,000 men. They were a motley, mixed company, made up of training companies, lower grade soldiers, including two 'ear battalions' men suffering from ear complaints, *Volkssturm*, and men from the SS training division stationed at the nearby infantry training school at Senne.

While the SS men were inexperienced and young, they were of good quality and gave a good account of themselves

83

wherever they appeared. The remainder, with the exception of the men of an officers training course employed north of Bielefeld, were less impressive. They panicked easily and were inclined to desert or withdraw whenever the action got too tough. In addition they were poorly equipped with foreign weapons, for which there was not sufficient ammunition, and were entrenched in hastily prepared positions which were hardly proof against the overwhelming weight of the Allied armoured thrust. Moreover these positions did not form a continuous line but were situated on the more important heights in the wooded feature to guard the passes which the Americans must cross if they wished to push on to the Weser. Even here the Germans had hardly any heavy weapons and no artillery at all. Their only defence against the American tanks was the cheap, easily manufactured, one-shot suicide weapon, the *panzerfaust*.

By the middle part of the morning of

Above left and left: The *Volksturm,* the people's army, composed of the unfit and very old. *Above:* The child-warriors are mobilised

2nd April, the leading American units were beginning to approach the foot of the *Teutoburger Wald,* groping their way cautiously, suspecting that the hills up ahead were dangerous, in spite of the ease with which they were capturing the small towns and villages that led up to the heights. To the left of the autobahn, two infantry divisions, the 84th Infantry and the 102nd, led by the 5th Armored Division were poised between Halle and Brackwede for the attack, while on the autobahn itself and to the right from Brackwede to Augustdorf, the 30th and 83rd Infantry Divisions plus the 2nd Armored were ready to go.

Faced with this situation, Becher, accompanied by his aide Major Düppenbedker, requested the local Nazi party bosses in Bielefeld to give him new *Volkssturm* units and dis-

tribute all food supplies to the local civilian populace. The drunken Nazis, safe in their concrete 'command bunker' accused him of being a traitor and threatened to have him 'strung up' there and then. Becher went back to his command and the Nazis took no further part in the proceedings. Two days later when a *Volkssturm* battalion commander reported to the still drunken party bosses that he needed further help, he was told that he had two rifles with five cartridges per rifle. That 'means ten dead Americans! . . Fight to the last man', they told him.

The Americans struck Becher's line on the night of 2nd/3rd April. Preceded by a low-level attack by the dreaded Allied fighter bombers, the Ninth attacked along the whole XII and XIV Corps area. To the north of the autobahn, resistance, on the whole, was light and easily overcome. Colonel Gilbert Farrand, Chief of Staff of the 5th Armored Division, recalls, 'The advance was really nothing more than cracking rear guard actions.' Even so Farrand's own half track, which he was using as the division's headquarters because of the rapidity of the advance, was hit by an enemy shell at this time. Enemy operations were conducted mainly on guerrilla lines rather than from a firm front.

The Germans would allow the American armour to penetrate their front and then wait for the slow moving infantry to approach, working their way cautiously through the wooded heights of the *Teutoburger Wald*. These Germans, usually small groups of fanatical SS-men or teenage Hitler youths, would launch a sudden attack on the Americans and after accounting for a dozen casualties would disappear as quickly as they had appeared. When trapped, as they mostly were in the end, they fought their positions to the last man, or perhaps a more appropriate expression would be last child. In several instances, the defenders to the north of

Ninth Army Tanks of 5th Armored Division drive towards Hameln

the autobahn turned out to be mere children. Lieutenant-Colonel Roland Kolb of the 84th Division noted that in one case his men were opposed by an 'artillery unit' manned by boys of twelve and under who 'rather than surrender fought until killed'.

The Americans reached the first pass through the *Teutoburger Wald* around midday when they started to attack south of Borgholzhausen, advancing from Halle. The pass was defended by a SS detachment and one or two companies of Wehrmacht soldiers under the command of a SS major, who had brought four anti-tank guns with him when he took over the assorted unit on 1st April.

The Americans began the attack with an armoured thrust, which bogged down a little in the narrow twisting roads and took some three hours to reach its objective. After suffering some twenty dead, the Germans withdrew in the direction of the small town of Melle. The pass was free and the road north, albeit a poor one, was open to the traffic which now began to pour through the woods and into the plain beyond. It was a cheap

victory bought at the cost of a handful of American dead and wounded.

To the south of the autobahn, however, resistance was stiffer and the US XIX Corps was involved in relatively heavy fighting between the old residential town of Detmold and Bielefeld itself. Just south of Detmold, fanatical SS men and young Wehrmacht recruits with no more than a couple of months' military training, fought desperately for every inch of ground, making up for their lack of heavy weapons by using the hilly wooded nature of the terrain which favoured the defender.

The village of Augustdorf was defended to the last man, and after it was taken, the Americans commenced their march to Detmold some six or seven miles away. They were met by a small group of German soldiers entrenched around one of Germany's holiest national monuments, *das Hermannsdenkmal*. Here under the massive metal monument set on a dominating height and crowned by the gigantic figure of Hermann the German, who in 9 AD supposedly defeated two Roman legions under Varus at this spot, the handful of German youths tried to emulate the feat of their forefathers. However their last ditch stand ended with their own deaths.

To the north of Augustdorf, another group of determined Germans succeeded in holding the pass at Oerlinghausen and stopped the American attack in the southern part of the little town itself. Although the Americans succeeded in capturing the southern part of the town after bitter house to house fighting, the German defenders still held the other half and the heights. In fact, on the evening of the 2nd, the Germans went over to the counter-offensive but were stopped dead by bitter US resistance. For the rest of that night both sides dug in and waited for the morning which would inevitably bring fresh American attacks.

Meanwhile the Americans had struck the German defences at Lämmershagen, the pass on the autobahn, which was defended by an infantry training battalion and by young officer cadets from an officer training course. While the American

tanks left the autobahn and tried to outflank the German positions, armoured cars felt their way along until they struck enemy resistance. Then infantry came up and tried to carry the German positions. When this attempt failed due to the obstinate resistance of the defenders, the Americans withdrew and brought down heavy fire on the German positions, guided by airborne artillery observers.

Towards evening the Shermans increased their fire and under its cover another group of tanks attacked, causing heavy losses among the enemy. About that time one group of tanks broke through, turned northwards along the top of the hills and dug themselves in for the night to the right of the pass. The Germans in that area began to withdraw to the village of Hillegossen, defended by officer cadets, where they waited for the dawn and fresh American attacks. This meant that the Americans had broken through but did not have control of the Hillegossen position. They knew that without this their traffic passing northwards along the autobahn to the Weser would always be threatened. Hillegossen, in other words, had to be taken.

On the morning of Tuesday, 3rd April, American troops opened a fresh attack on both Hillegossen and the heights around Oerlinghausen. Under artillery cover, a combined tank and infantry group attempted to rush the defenders of the Hillegossen position. This time they succeeded. The Germans began to withdraw, retreating into the protection of the woods and from there in the general direction of the Weser. By midday truck after truck was rolling down the autobahn northwards.

The battle for the Oerlinghausen positions was not so easy. It lasted most of the day with seventy-one casualties on the German side and perhaps a score on the American side. At about four o'clock in the afternoon the German defenders of the Panzer Grenadier Training Bat-

talion 64, who had defended the position with little else than their rifles and machine guns, started to retire northwards, followed by a long column of American armoured vehicles eager to get to the Weser. One King Tiger had appeared in the area but it had been knocked out by a German soldier by mistake! The enraged SS occupants of the tank thereupon shot the wretched infantryman who had put them out of action.

Now the German defenders began to give way everywhere. General Becher left Bielefeld and took up his headquarters in the area of the River Weser. To the left of the autobahn all resistance was overcome by the late evening of the 3rd. Bielefeld itself still held out, though the Americans had not yet attempted to make a serious attack on the town itself but contented themselves with probing attacks on its suburbs to the south, west and east. To the right of the autobahn the Germans still held out along the heights of the *Teutoburger Wald*, though as we have seen the pass at Oerlinghausen had been seized. At Detmold, the next largest town in the area, the Americans still were held up.

The Ninth Army command ordered up the tactical air force. After a preliminary artillery bombardment and a brief air raid by Allied fighter bombers dropping incendiaries, the leading unit of the 2nd Armored Division was ready to attack.

As the first tanks of the 82nd Reconnaissance Battalion began to enter the suburbs of the medieval city, which had once been the home of local princes, a civilian met them and announced that the owner of the local armament plant, one of Germany's largest, wished to surrender.

While shells fell all around him, Colonel Merriam, the commander of the Reconnaissance Battalion, received the surrender of the plant in a ceremony, complete with a formal speech and the gift of the owner's chromed pistol, which was slightly absurd in the light of the circum-

Above: Hangar at Detmold suffers heavy damage from US bombing before the town's capture. *Below:* The entry of 2nd Armored Division, Ninth US Army, into Lemgo

stances under which it took place. Then he passed on to take the surrender of a German paymaster company, which had in its possession vast quantities of *Reichmarks*. Believing that Detmold was taken and that his battalion had the situation well in hand, Merriam ordered the advance to the Weser to continue.

Only a few hours later, armoured infantry coming up behind Merriam had to deploy and fight a bitter frustrating battle against SS units which had dug themselves in and about the town. What happened at Detmold that day was typical of the confused fighting south of the autobahn on the 4th and 5th April. After the war General Macon, commanding general of the 83rd Infantry Division, recalled 'walking quite safely through the front entrance of my headquarters, but when I tried to leave by the back door, I almost had to fight my way out.'

In some places the Germans, sick of the destruction and death all about them, surrendered without a fight. At Lemgo, for example, the local *bürgermeister* Wilhelm Graefer drove through the German lines and surrendered his city to Colonel Hugh Farrell of the 2nd Division, only to be shot for his pains after a thirty minutes trial by command of Major-General Paul Goerbig one day later. In other places, the Americans tricked the local German leaders into surrendering without a shot. Captain Francis Schommer of the 83rd Division, a fluent German speaker, used his linguistic gifts and the threat of his forty-five calibre pistol to convince the *bürgermeister* of any newly captured town to telephone his colleague in the next town on the division's line of advance. Schommer would say: 'If he wants the place to remain standing, he'd better surrender it right now. Tell him to get the people to hang sheets from their windows – or else.' The panic-stricken local mayor would thereupon usually pour it on, telling his neighbour that the Americans in his town

had hundreds of tanks and artillery pieces, and thousands upon thousands of troops. The ruse worked again and again.'

Thus the Americans pressed forward all along the line. South of Bielefeld, the *bürgermeister* of the little town of Brackwede, Herr Bitter, ordered the tank barricades to be removed from the road leading into Bielefeld so that the Americans might enter without a fight. On the day before the Americans reached his little town, he was arrested and shot at the order of the local party boss. Still the Americans managed to take Brackwede without any serious fighting. The opposition around the town began to collapse. The defence possessed two tanks only and one of these could not be moved. The locally recruited units began to acquire civilian clothes and disappear. Colonel Sommer quickly realised that the only troops he could rely upon were those defending the autobahn outside the town and the young experienced men of a reserve officers' course employed to the north of Bielefeld and linked with the defenders of the autobahn pass.

At 1300 hours on the 4th April, the first American tanks entered Bielefeld. Approaching the first barrier on the road from the south they were hit by fire from German bazookas. Hurriedly they withdrew and started firing at the German defenders hidden somewhere in the neighbouring houses. All afternoon the firing continued sporadically until five hours later a strong armoured force broke through and headed for the 'Sedan Bunker', which supposedly still housed the head of the local Nazi party and his staff. But the Bielefeld Nazis had flown towards the east and safety, leaving the citizens to their fate. These people seized the opportunity at last presented to them and began to plunder the local military supply depots, while others quickly hoisted the white flag of surrender 'over the town hall. The battle, if it can be called a battle, for Bielefeld was finally over.

Meanwhile the fight for the passes through the *Teutoburger Wald* continued and with it all the horror of war. Approaching one of the wooded ridges, Major James Hollingworth of the 2nd Division's 67th Armored Regiment, suddenly found himself surrounded by what appeared to be German tanks. Fortunately for him, the tanks were relics without engines so that they were not mobile. All the same they still had their deadly eighty-eight millimetre guns. Swiftly the young German gunners opened up.

Hollingworth's gunner, Staff-Sergeant Cooley, replied almost at once. Swinging his seventy-five millimetre gun, he knocked out the first German at a range of 1,500 yards. Desperately operating the electrical turret mechanism, he fired at another relic less than seventy-five yards away. Then, as Hollingworth remembers, 'all hell broke loose.'

The superiority of manoeuvre and firepower was on the side of the 67th Armored and it did not take the Americans long to get the situation under control. Unfortunately, however, just as they had finished off the German opposition, a German truck came rumbling down the road towards their positions. Hollingworth ordered his men to hold their fire until the unsuspecting truck had approached within seventy yards of the American positions. Then at point blank range, he gave the command to open fire. The tankers poured machine gun fire into the vehicle's open sides. The truck came to a halt, burst into flames and overturned, spilling its dead and dying occupants onto the road. It was only some minutes later when Hollingworth went across to look at his kill, that he found to his horror that the truck had been filled with *Flakhelferinnen*, German women soldiers employed in the anti-aircraft service.

Thus the Ninth Army pushed through the *Teutoburger Wald* and the drive north east began to gather

More prisoners of Ninth Army

The army crosses the Weser at Minden

momentum. Prisoners started to pour in. Unescorted and exhausted, thousands of German POWs began the long trudge southwards to prison cages waiting for them on the Rhine, while the roads going the other way were jammed with thousands of olive drab vehicles hurrying towards the River Weser. By the evening of 4th April, six American divisions (two infantry and one armoured north of the autobahn and two infantry and one armoured south of it) were through the wooded hills and on their way to the last river barrier before the Elbe itself.

Meanwhile to the south east of the Ninth Army, General Hodges' First Army had been making steady progress in its drive towards the Weser. Well up in front the veteran 2nd Infantry Division had captured the large town of Hofgeismar on the night of 3rd April. The town, situated some fifteen miles from the river, fell only after a determined fight against the SS garrison. The next morning, the 1st Battalion of the Division's 23rd Infantry Regiment attacked and captured the small town of Karlsdorf, pushing on along a secondary road to Hombressen, only a few miles from the Weser.

Opposition was light. The infantry column was attacked from the flank by three Mark IVs, but these soon fled when one of their number was hit from over a mile away by a lucky shot from one of the American tank destroyers. The infantry pressed on again and were halted only momentarily at the outskirts of Hombressen when an American tank was hit by German fire from some nearby woods. The advance continued. By nightfall, the leading battalion of the 23rd Infantry had reached the town of Veckerhagen on the western bank of the Weser.

There the infantry were allowed to eat quickly, before they were issued with ammunition and food for two days and sent down to the river. Opposite them on the eastern bank was the small town of Hameln and

beyond it the ground rose abruptly into cliff-like hills. The town and the river looked a tough objective to take, but surprisingly enough the 2nd Infantry Division achieved their aim with remarkable ease. The First Battalion, which had met little resistance through the woods to Veckerhagen and had reached the river first, radioed regimental headquarters that there seemed to be no opposition on the other side. As a result E and F Companies of the First's sister battalion, which were experiencing some trouble near Hombressen, were pulled out and sent across the river in assault boats.

The enemy did not fire a shot. The river was undefended. The only casualties the 2nd Division suffered came just as the infantrymen reached the town of Hameln when divisional artillery fire fell short and landed among the assault troops. One man was killed and another lost his leg. The first crossing of the River Weser by troops of Hodges' First Army cost him exactly two men.

The Ninth was not so lucky. Reaching the Weser between Minden and another Hamelin (of Pied Piper fame), the XII and XIX Corps made fierce attempts to seize a bridge across the 225-foot river. Although their efforts were inspired by an urgent desire to get across and on to the Elbe, from whence they hoped to attack Berlin, the Americans failed to seize a bridge. The result was that the Ninth had to carry out an assault crossing near Hameln in the early morning of 5th April. Opposition was limited to small arms fire and the lead tanks of the 2nd Armored Division bypassed the pockets of resistance left in the ancient town itself. But the following soldiers of the 30th Infantry Division were forced to fight intensively to overcome the suicidal resistance offered by small isolated groups of SS men.

While other Ninth Army men paddled silently across the river during the night, the 30th Division

was forced to call up the whole weight of the divisional artillery. The American guns began their deadly work of destruction and by the time they had finished on the 5th April, the old city of cobbled streets and half-timbered houses was blasted into a pile of smoking rubble. As Colonel Walter Johnson of the 117th Regiment said somewhat cynically: 'This time we got the rats out with a slightly different kind of flute!'

Thus on the 5th April, the two armies, Ninth and First, were able to commence the last stage of their race east to isolate the Harz and reach the Elbe. The Ninth met little resistance because the 47 Panzer Corps which was expected to defend the Weser area was trapped in the Ruhr pocket and most of the First Parachute Army was being pushed back by the British 2nd Army. This allowed the Ninth to advance across the low rolling country north of the hills whilst the First crossed the wide Thuringian plain to their south.

In three days time on 8th April,

On the last stage of the race east

Kesselring ordered the River Leine to be defended 'under all circumstances', but the Americans had already crossed it and begun to fan out on both sides of the Harz, where General Lucht's Eleventh Army was now trapped without heavy weapons or much food and ammunition. The Germans' only advantage was the nature of the terrain. Although General Wenck's Twelfth Army did open an abortive campaign a few days later to relieve the Harz and presumably to penetrate from thence into the Ruhr and relieve Model, that is no longer part of our story. By the first week of April 1945 it was clear that the fate of Army Group B was virtually sealed. The Harz itself was isolated and there was no space to its front from which the Germans could launch an armoured or mobile counter attack. Any hope of a successful outcome to Model's defence of the Ruhr would now have to come from Model himself and the men under his command.

Attack into the Pocket

On 2nd April, the day the pocket was finally closed, representatives of the First and Ninth Armies met to discuss the strategy for closing the 'sack', as the GIs would soon be calling the Ruhr Kessel. At their conference the staff officers of the two armies established the Ruhr river, running from Nuttlar south of the link-up point down to where it joined the Rhine at Duisburg, as the dividing line between the First and the Ninth. They would attack towards this geographical feature with the equivalent of four corps in a converging movement.

The Ninth Army's zone of operations, the northern part of the Ruhr, was the smaller of the two, but it was a congested industrial area with one grimy depressing city hardly distinguishable from another. In some instances these cities were so close to one another that it was hard to tell where one ended and another began. The locals had often boasted before the war that it was possible to move across the whole Ruhr complex by tramcar. In cities such as Essen, Dortmund and Duisburg, it was most likely that the Ninth Army could expect a bitter plodding battle with house to house fighting through the bombed streets unless the German defence collapsed abruptly. And at this time there seemed no likelihood of that happening.

Model had some of his best remaining divisions left in the area. Under the command of the dedicated Nazi Colonel-General Harpe, who had succeeded von Manteuffel in the leadership of the battle-hardened Fifth Panzer Army, the enemy had three corps spread out in the area: the XII SS Corps on the right, the LXXXI in the centre and the LVII Panzer Corps to the left. They presented formidable opposition. In addition to the ruined cities already mentioned, they had to their right the Ruhr canal system including the Dortmund-Ems Canal running north to south and covering the front of many of the Ruhr cities; while to their south was the

Colonel-General Harpe

Rhine itself. In truth, the Ninth Army's task would not be easy.

As for the First Army, its area south of the Ruhr river was three times as large as that of the Ninth. Apart from the industrial centres of Düsseldorf, once the fashion capital of Germany, Wuppertal and the eastern suburbs of Cologne, it was about eighty per cent forested. It consisted mainly of the hilly, isolated Sauerland the name of which gives a clue to the inhospitable and infertile nature of the terrain. With its dense woods, tight winding valleys, poor roads and many deep, fast flowing streams, the area was ideally suited for defence and a delaying action by even a small force.

But in spite of the many problems facing them that day, the staff officers of the two armies agreed to go ahead with their task. One corps of the Ninth Army would attack on 4th April and attempt an assault crossing of the canal system, in particular the Rhine-Herne and Dortmund-Ems Canals. One day later the second corps of the Ninth Army, the XIX Corps, would attempt to break out further north in the Lippstadt area, its objective being the key communications centre of Soest. Once this corps had broken through and reached the Ruhr river it would swing southwards along the

Anderson, Simpson and Churchill on his visit to the front east of the Rhine

right bank of the river and link up with the XVI Corps, which the staff officers presumed would by then be involved in the battle for the Ruhr cities.

On the 5th April, the First Army would also launch an attack, its objective being a decisive breakthrough across the River Sieg, followed by a powerful drive on a two corps front towards the Ruhr river where the First would link up with the Ninth.

Meanwhile General Gerow's Fifteenth Army guarding the west bank of the Rhine between Bonn and Duisburg with three infantry divisions would ensure that the German defenders on the far bank did not use patrols or paratroops to interfere with Allied traffic and communications. They would also keep substantial German forces pinned down in the area by aggressive patrols across the waterway into German territory.

On the 3rd April, Major-General John Anderson's XVI Corps began to assemble around the recently captured town of Recklinghausen preparatory to the assault on the Ruhr canal system, Andersen would attack into the pocket with three divisions on a thirty-seven mile front along the Rhine-Herne Canal between the River

Lippe in the north and the Rhine in the south. The divisions would be: the 79th in the south, the 35th in the centre and the 75th, with the 116th Regiment of the 29th Division under command, in the north.

The operation meant the crossing of several canals including the formidable Dortmund-Ems on the 75th Division's front. Here the canal was thirty feet deep with perpendicular sides, and although the waterway had been drained it still contained three feet of water and mud in its thirty-five yard breadth. If that was not enough, the division's advance was hampered by subsidiary canals.

Defending the canal system in 16 sector were the remnants of the 2nd Paratroop Division, which had done sterling work in the March Rhineland fighting and was now reduced to some 4,000 men. It occupied the area south of the Rhine-Herne Canal from the Rhine to Gelsenkirchen. The line was continued to the vicinity of the Zweig Canal by the 190th Volksgrenadier Division with about 3,500 men. The rest of the line was held by the 18th Volksgrenadier Division of 2,000 men.

On the 3rd April the 75th Infantry Division began to send combat patrols across the Dortmund-Ems Canal to test the enemy's strength and these

The Ruhr in ruins. *Above:* Monorail has collapsed into the Wupper river near Wuppertal. *Below:* These tank turrets in the yards at Aschaffenburg will never be delivered

succeeded, surprisingly enough, in establishing a small bridgehead on the division's left flank. One company even managed to penetrate the enemy line on the far bank and return with fifty-five prisoners. While this minor preliminary action was going on, the 35th and 79th Divisions continued to maintain and improve their positions along the northern bank of the Rhine-Herne Canal preparatory to the assault of the morrow.

The assault began at 0100 hours on 4th April with the three regiments of the 75th Division, plus the 116th Regiment of the 29th, crossing the Dortmund-Ems Canal in line abreast on a seven mile front. In the case of the 116 Regiment, the action of which was typical of the fighting that day, its line of advance was bounded on both flanks by two other minor canals. The regiment took up its position quickly on the left bank of the Dortmund-Ems Canal under heavy machine gun and mortar fire. Ladders were rushed up and the infantry began to descend into the muddy water below. Wading through the mud under heavy fire, the infantry threw their scaling ladders against the opposite bank, while their own machine gunners covered them with rapid fire which was so intensive that their ammunition soon gave out and they had to be supplied by a light plane which bravely landed in full view of the enemy.

Once on the other side, the advance bogged down a little, while the machine gunners replenished their ammunition and then continued under heavy enemy fire. But if the German machine gunners were prepared to fight to the end, the infantry, generally, were not and there were signs everywhere that the Germans were weakening.

Meanwhile engineers from the 75th Division tried to fill in the canal by bulldozing and exploding the walls of the waterway into the muddy mess below. But their efforts failed. The concrete walls were reinforced by steel wire. The 116th pushed on. A reconnaissance party discovered that a bridge still remained intact over the canal east of the Lippe Canal, which ran along the Regiment's left flank. Colonel Bingham, the Regiment's CO immediately ordered the development of a crossing site on the Lippe Canal to provide an entrance into the right zone. Engineers of the 75th Division obliged, and this time they discovered that the walls of the Lippe Canal were *not* reinforced. They pushed in the walls with their bulldozers and the infantry were able to pass. By the end of the day, the 116th Infantry had overrun the town of Waltrop, and had dug in along lines four miles beyond the canal. As dusk fell armour began to cross over the bridge and the Lippe Canal where the engineers had filled it in.

Meanwhile the efforts of the 75th Division had also met with success. It had attacked with three regiments abreast of each other. The 291st had met little opposition in the northern sector of the division's front, but the 289th Regiment in the south advanced under intense fire. In the end, however, the regiment succeeded in penetrating into the outskirts of the small town of Ickern and finally cleared it by the evening of the same day. When dusk fell that day the 75th Division and its attached regiment the 116th Infantry were firmly established along a seven mile front to a depth of five miles.

Now the cities of the Ruhr loomed in front of them. These once great centres of population, ruined by years of bombing, lay gaunt and broken in the fog of war, a suitable backdrop for the last act of the tragedy. With their great slag heaps, tortured railway tracks and shattered buildings they waited for the final assault to come. General von Mellenthin of the Fifth Panzer Army wrote: 'I have seen many battlefields but none so strange as the great industrial complex of the Ruhr during the final destruction of Army Group B.'

But the eager Americans had no

time to reflect upon either the tragedy of war or the strangeness of the battlefield against which it was set. Further north, the XIX Corps had also gone over to the offensive with the 8th Armored Division driving for the town of Soest against stiff opposition from the elite and experienced 116th Panzer Division. Under the command of General von Waldenburg, the division had not done too well in Normandy but it had successfully spearheaded the Ardennes push as part of Manteuffel's Fifth Panzer Army. Now it fought well, retreating only when absolutely necessary and making the Americans pay for every foot of ground they gained. At times it launched counter attacks in the Hamm area, presumably to try to open a new escape route for the German Army Group. Time and time again, the German division launched local attacks, mostly at night, probing for weak spots in the American line.

In the end Major-General Raymond McLain, commanding XIX Corps, was forced to order the 95th Division, positioned west of the 8th Armored, into action to help out and take the wind out of the German sails. On the 4th April the 95th Division attacked over the River Lippe. At first the assault went well, but then the Division's 378th Regiment, struck a hornet's nest at Hamm and had to call for air support. The XXIX Tactical Air Corps sent its fighter bombers roaring in at tree top level at the defenceless Germans, both at Hamm and Soest, knocking the heart out of them. By the end of the day they had started to surrender in droves.

The advance picked up again. Further south, the 35th and 79th Divisions prepared to cross their sections of the canal system, while the 95th Division and the 8th Armored Division began to converge on the key communications centre of Soest.

As the Ninth Army fought closer

Troops cross the track at the marshalling yards at Hamm

and closer to the industrial complex west of the Ruhr river, the First Army east of the river had begun its offensive on the Fifth. On a two corps front, Collins' VII and Ridgway's XVIII Corps, the First Army attacked into the pocket from the south and the east.

In the VII Corps area, the advance had been stalled in the Winterberg sector by the Germans' insistence on holding the Meschede-Brilon roadway system as a last means of breaking out of the Ruhr trap. Now the corps determined to force the enemy line back beyond Meschede. One of the first attempts to do this was made by Task Force Birks, composed of Combat Command A of the 7th Armored Division and the 47th Infantry

A soldier watches for snipers, Hamm

Regiment of the 9th Division, and commanded by the assistant divisional commander of the 9th, Brigadier-General Hammond Birks.

On 5th April, this force attacked from the area of Niedersfeld and pushed ahead rapidly despite heavy opposition, the worst being met in the hilly region south west of the small town of Wiemeringshausen. Here, where the terrain was unsuitable for the CCA's tanks, the unaccompanied infantry was subjected to heavy 20mm and machine gun fire. But Birks urged his men on and by nightfall on that day, his force had taken six small towns and pressed as far north as Elleringhausen. Meanwhile the rest of the 9th Division attacked north and north west, advancing up the road from Winterberg, capturing the small towns of Silbach and Siedlingshausen,

as they drove towards the resort town of Brilon some twenty miles north east of Meschede.

Further south in the XVIII Airborne Corps' area, the 78th Infantry Division with the 8th Infantry Division to its right had crossed the Sieg, swollen by the spring rains, and were advancing against remnants of the 62nd, 59th and 363rd Volksgrenadier Divisions plus the 11th Panzer, a total of some 10,000 men.

In the first day of the advance, which had as its final objective the town of Wuppertal, some fifty miles from the corps' starting point, the Americans met stiff resistance. Taking full advantage of the rugged terrain, ideally suited for defence, the Germans defended virtually every village and town, destroying bridges, road and railways as they retreated.

But after about forty-eight hours of combat, the Americans' overwhelming superiority began to tell and the Germans' resistance started to weaken. Now the triumphant XVIII Airborne Corps realised that only the main roads and important junctions were being defended. The Germans were surrendering in ever increasing numbers, in some cases almost begging to be taken prisoner.

Thus it was that by dusk on 7th April, the American advance was successful everywhere. They had stopped the attempts of Army Group B to break out to both east and west and were themselves pushing ever deeper into the pocket, after breaching the canal system and the River Sieg lines. On that day the main centres of

Troops by-pass a road block, Hamm

Left: Field Artillery battalion moves through wreckage of Essen
Above: Remschied. *Below:* The 605th Tank Destroyer Battalion wait to relieve Company C of the same unit, Mulheim

Sniper search in the ruins of the Krupp works, Essen

German resistance were located in such cities as Dortmund, Essen, Düsseldorf, Remscheid and Hagen sited between the Ruhr and Wupper rivers. These cities, which before the war had housed many hundreds of thousands of people, were all huge complexes of factories, mines and dwelling areas, capable of swallowing infantry divisions by the dozen. In addition, because of the ruined nature of these Ruhr towns, Allied armoured superiority would be of little use to them in the house to house fighting that would soon develop. Nor would the Air Force be of much use as the infantry commanders feared that any large scale bombing attack on these towns would be just as likely to strike their own men as the enemy. In fact, virtually all air operations against targets in the Ruhr were soon to be stopped.

Formidable objectives as these Ruhr towns were, their resources were low. In most cases public transport had ceased. Electricity and gas had been cut off by Allied bombing or shell fire. Food was scarce and water obtained only from communal taps. Most of the remaining populace spent their days huddled in candle-lit cellars, venturing out into the grey ruined horror of the streets only when hunger or thirst forced them to. These last civilians, caught up unwillingly in the middle of a great battle, were broken creatures, destroyed by six years of bombing and privation. Now all they wanted was an end to the terror.

But if the civilian populace of these ruined towns was ready to give in, their military defenders were not. Dug in among the still smoking ruins, fanatical remnants of SS units, who had nothing more to lose except their lives, and paratroopers, who were skilled in the execution of these last-ditch stands, waited and prepared to give battle. The fight for the cities was about to begin.

Die Wacht am Rhein

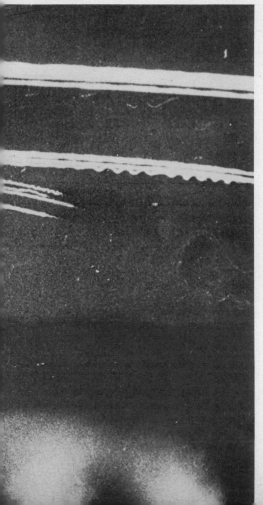

For over a week while the fighting had been going on to the north, the three infantry divisions of General Gerow's Fifteenth Army, guarding the Rhine from Bonn to Cologne and from there to the point south east of Duisberg where they linked up with the Ninth Army, had been watching the opposite bank of the river. Searching the enemy positions on the other side of the broad expanse of water by field glasses during the day and by means of searchlights at night, they had tried to ascertain his strength and his intentions. But the Germans had proved themselves very elusive and there had been little evidence of their presence save for an occasional burst of machine gun fire from some irate gunner or the rare mortar 'stonk' when some careless truck driver or platoon commander presented an all too obvious target on the US side of the great river.

Some officers at divisional headquarters thought that the Germans had drained the Rhine front to reinforce the fronts to east and west now under severe attack by the First and Ninth Armies. Others were of the opinion that there were plenty of Germans lying low in well-concealed positions on the other side of the river, waiting for the Americans to make

Above: First Army troops fire over the river on German positions
Below: On the other side Germans watch for movements. *Below right:* Allied airborne troops drop east of the Rhine

the first move. Thus the opinions conflicted, and as the first week of April came to an end, the three divisions involved, the inexperienced 94th Infantry, and the veteran 82nd and 101st Airborne Divisions, started to send more and more patrols across the waterway. Perhaps their commanders thought in addition to gaining information from these patrols, they would also force the Germans to withdraw men from the other two fronts to strengthen their positions along the Rhine. Perhaps they only wanted to ensure that their men did not grow stale on this inactive front, especially the veteran paratroopers who had a bad habit of getting into serious trouble once they were out of action and had time on their hands. Events in England, France and Holland had shown this to be true time and time again.

Whatever reasons the commanders gave themselves and their subordinates to justify the increased patrol activity during the second week of April, they began that week to raise the number and the strength of the combat patrols which started to slip across the river, mostly at night or in the early morning. At first most of the patrols succeeded in getting across with little difficulty, and if they did not bring back much information, they did not at least incur any great casualties. However, this situation was soon to change.

The 82nd Airborne Division, veteran of Sicily and Holland, was the first of Gerow's three divisions to encounter the increased German resistance on the Rhine front. On the morning of 6th April at 0230 hours, A Company of the 504 Parachute Regiment began to cross the Rhine steathily in their assault boats. Their task was to seize and hold the village of Hitdorf, some miles north of Cologne. This village was to be used as a bridgehead, not for offensive action deeper into enemy territory, but solely to draw further

enemy troops into the area.

The 140 men of the company landed safely enough. But almost immediately they ran into trouble. Under heavy artillery fire which suddenly descended upon them, they ran into a minefield in the darkness and in the ensuing confusion, broke up into two groups without contact with the Company HQ. All the same the two separated units fought their way to the objective, striking through a roadblock and a machine gun nest until finally by 0830 hours, they had rejoined and taken Hitdorf with a gain of 68 prisoners.

The tired but happy paratroopers thought they had the situation well in hand and were preparing to settle down in their newly won positions, when the German counter attack hit them only fifteen minutes after they had finally cleared the village. German infantry rushed them and without giving the veterans of the 82nd Airborne time to dig in their heels, threw them out of the village until finally the steam left the German assault and the Americans could bring them to a halt.

But only for a while. Shortly afterwards the Germans came again. Preceded by a brief but heavy artillery bombardment, which knocked out all the Company's wireless communications and their OP post which was still located in the steeple of the village church, the Germans covered their approach with smoke and attacked with two tanks and a company of infantry. By means of signals the paratroopers called down their own artillery from the far bank of the Rhine. The resultant fire scattered the German battle line for a while. But the enemy regrouped and pressed home their attack with a will.

The paratroopers' 3rd Platoon was overrun and wiped out. German tanks, supported by infantry, started to advance through the village while 200 infantry came in from the north. Two platoons were overrun and cut off almost immediately. Outgunned and decidedly outnumbered, the Americans started to withdraw to the beaches, fighting as they went. Here two platoons established a horseshoe defence with its open end facing the water and waited for the enemy to hit them in strength. Aware now of the gravity of A Company's position on the other side of the Rhine, regimental headquarters realised that it must do something, and do it soon, if A Company was not to be wiped out.

At 0130 hours, I Company crossed the river and began to support the survivors of its fellow unit. The Germans attacked with a platoon of Mark IVs and about 300 infantry. The attack was repulsed with some difficulty but a paratrooper did succeed in knocking out a Mark IV with a gammon bomb. Now the new company went over to the attack and catching the Germans off guard managed to clear the beachhead temporarily of the enemy. They then withdrew, followed shortly afterwards by what was left of Company A.

Later it was estimated that the raid had killed and wounded some 350 Germans and resulted in eighty prisoners, but all the same it had cost A Company nine dead, seventy-nine missing and twenty-four wounded. In other words, almost the whole company was put out of action. As the divisional history later put it: 'In view of the high casualties it was difficult to say that the mission was a success. From the viewpoint of these GIs involved, the operation was a miniature 'Dunkirk' with at most a hollow satisfaction. Fighting men don't believe in moral victories.'

For a while patrol activity came almost to an end on the Rhine after the 82nd's bad experience, but a few days later the inexperienced 94th Division decided to try its hand at the game.

Under the command of Lt Seeby, a group of twenty men was sent across

A paratrooper presses forward to outflank an enemy position

Infantry ride a tank of 9th Armored Division, First Army, in the advance

the river at Serm near Krefeld. Its objective was to move north of Angermund to determine whether there were any Germans in the area. Skirting the town, the patrol advanced cautiously towards its objective when it was suddenly struck by German fire.

Staff-Sergeant Jerome Fatora, who was the senior NCO with the patrol, describes what followed in this manner: 'The Heinies brought 40mm AA fire to bear on the route we used to enter the area. Simultaneously other Krauts on the right and left, working with clocklike precision, were manoeuvring to outflank us, while keeping us hemmed in by fire. Consequently Lt Seeby decided to regroup the patrol for better defense and to take advantage of some shrubbery in the vicinity. Using the old infantry "fire and movement", we managed to reach a house around which we planned to build a defense.'

Reaching the house safely, the American patrol set up its defence and shortly afterwards found itself surrounded by the Germans. Night fell and the Germans started to press home their advantage, creeping closer

and closer to the house.

'Frequently during the night,' Sergeant Fatora explained, 'we were asked to surrender only to reply with hot lead. Bazookas smashed the house and machine guns raked all the doors and windows . . . Early next morning after several attempts to escape had proved futile and the Heinies had battered the cellar entrance with panzerfausts we gave up all hope of escape. About eight o'clock in the morning the Jerries, numbering seventy-five in all,rushed the house. In a melodramatic speech, their Lieutenant shouted to us in perfect English 'Gentlemen (all of a sudden he

considered us gentlemen) you have five minutes to surrender.'

'Surrender to us,' cried Lt Seeby.

'Sir,' cracked his reply, 'I am a soldier and as such I have my orders which I must obey. You have four minutes.'

'But you are already caught in the center of a huge pincers.'

'My men and I realise that but we have superiors over us to whom we must answer and anyway,' he hesitated a few seconds, 'you will be prisoners of war only a few days before you are freed by your comrades. You have two minutes left.'

All the time Pfc White had been trying to repair the patrol's defective radio. Finally he made it and managed to contact the battalion command post. While he was so occupied, the German officer shouted again 'You have one minute remaining. You are surrounded.'

At that moment, the radio went dead again.

The German shouted. 'Your time is up gentlemen. Are you coming out?' As Fatora describes it: 'Silence fell on the room as Lt Seeby said:"Yeahwe're coming out." '

The men of the 94th Division marched into the prison camp to be rescued a few days later by the 13th Armored Division as the German officer had predicted.

After this episode, patrol activity across the Rhine died down, the airborne divisions consolidated their resources and prepared for any operational order that might come their way. The 94th Infantry contented itself with occasional mortar and machine gun duels with their opponents across the Rhine. Even these began to die away as the Germans started to feel the pressure exerted by the First Army's 13th Armored Division bearing down on the Rhine near Cologne in the east and the 303rd Infantry Regiment of the 97th Division on the Ninth Army's front, approaching Baumberg north west of the great Rhenish city.

The last
battle

On the 9th April, all Ninth Army units engaged in the reduction of the Ruhr Pocket came under the command of XVI Corps. Thus a total of one armoured, five infantry and one airborne division (the 17th) came under Major-General John Anderson's command while Major-General Raymond McLain's XIX Corps was finally freed for the drive eastwards.

Anderson brought under tighter control his scattered units, which had been dispersed in a score of minor and major battles for the approaches to the great cities of the Ruhr. He threw them forward in one final effort to destroy the last vestiges of German power north of the Ruhr river. The 35th Infantry Division attacked across the Rhine Herne Canal, north of Herne, at 0630 on that day and swiftly established two bridgeheads against scattered resistance to a depth of two miles along an eight miles front. Its 134th Regiment outflanked Gelsenkirchen along its eastern suburbs and finally entered the city. With the

pressure on its flanks eased by the efforts of the 17th Airborne and the fresh attack of the 35th Division that day, the 79th Division thrust rapidly south towards the Ruhr river, seizing Steele and cutting the German forces in the Ruhr into two swiftly closing pockets.

Meanwhile in front of the great industrial city of Dortmund, which before the war had had a population of nearly 600,000 inhabitants, the German forces attacked once more. Supported by heavy artillery fire, the Wehrmacht thrust forward north west of Dortmund across the Dortmund-Ems Canal, but the 75th Division, which was bearing the brunt of the fighting in the Dortmund area, managed to repulse them without any noticeable loss of ground. The 75th found that day that it was capable only of 'tidying up' the divisional area and clearing away the scattered pockets of resistance still to be found behind its line. It was incapable of doing more.

Below left: Guarding the Herne Canal. *Above and below:* Advance into Gelsenkirchen

Above: The intact Duisberg bridge. *Above right:* Mortar section moves through a rubble choked underpass in the advance on Dortmund

But help was on its way for the hard pressed 75th. A powerful task force, made up of the 95th Division, the 194th Glider Regiment of the 17th Airborne, and the 8th Armored, plus the 15th Cavalry Group, began to thrust on Dortmund from the east and sweep the foe before it towards the town itself. Pushing steadily forward that day, its objective was to link up with the 75th Division. By the end of the day this task force had finished mopping up resistance on its front, and had advanced within three miles of Unna. The 8th Armored was positioned in the small town of Wiekede, and the 15th Cavalry Group was located north of the Lippe River.

On the following day the 17th Airborne Division occupied the eastern part of Essen, home of the Krupp industries, without opposition. The 79th drove east between the 35th Division on the north and the Ruhr

river on the south and cleared Wattenscheid and the western half of Bochum. The net being drawn around Dortmund was being pulled tighter and tighter together.

The German command realised the American intention. Seeking to save the forces within the city of Dortmund from being trapped before they could be evacuated south of the Ruhr river, the enemy fought desperately as the 8th Armored and the 95th Divisions, advancing abreast of each other, thrust to within two miles of the link-up with the 75th Division.

The Germans attacked with several hundred infantry covered by a number of Tiger tanks. They went for the 8th Armored in a furious knock-about manner, but the tankers stood their ground that evening and brought the enemy to a standstill. When the steam had finally gone out of the German counter attack, the 8th advanced

again to within a mile of Unna and the outskirts of the town of Frondenberg, which lies to the south east of it. At the same time the 95th Division's 378th Regiment had advanced eight miles along the Lippe River while its sister regiment the 379th had entered Kamen and had fought its way to within a mile of Unna by evening.

On the 11th April the Americans pushed on against patchy resistance, sweeping the industrial Ruhr clear of German troops, except for the enemy bridgehead in the Dortmund area. It was a great day for American arms. The corps captured Mülheim, Oberhausen, Bochum, Unna and the remainder of Essen, seizing bridges intact across the River Ruhr at Mülheim, Witten and Kettwig and establishing positions along the banks of the river for forty two miles until it flowed into the Rhine in the vicinity of Witten. From Witten the corps' positions now ran east from Krondenberg to Arnsberg where it was in contact with the 1st Army's III Corps.

North of the Ruhr river the end was very near. Yet the fanatical garrison of the ruined city of Dortmund still held out obstinately, inspired perhaps by the fact that the Gestapo were beginning to shoot 'defeatists' and resistance workers in the city's parks.

Meanwhile the First Army had not been idle. On the day that the 9th completed its great sweep of the Ruhr cities, the 1st's 13th Armored Division swung into the town of Siegburg and headed for the eastern suburbs of Cologne, still held stubbornly by the 3rd Parachute Division, or what was left of it. The young paratroopers were manning the dreaded 88 s, once used as anti-aircraft weapons in the defence of the Ruhr's industrial cities. They fired into the advancing Shermans with everything they had. As always the American tanks with their high silhouettes and less powerful guns were ineffective against the German weapon. Tank after tank was hit and went up in flames or came to a sudden halt, tracks flipping forward

like broken limbs. That day the Germans knocked out thirty US tanks.

To the north of the 13th, other First Army troops had an easier day, advancing against little more than sniper fire. Gummersbach was captured, then Markenputz, where one regiment found itself the surprised owner of fifty million dollars' worth of Reichmarks discovered in the local bank. German resistance was crumbling more and more, but still in spite of the mass surrenders that were taking place everywhere, some German officers insisted that the traditional niceties of military etiquette should be observed.

The 2nd Battalion of the 309th Infantry Regiment (78th Division), for instance, was driving into the military hospital town of Lindlar when two German officers bearing white flags barred their way. They stated they wanted to declare the place an open city. They also reported that a lieutenant-general and his staff were waiting within the town to carry out a formal surrender ceremony. The battalion sent an officer to meet the German general, but when some time had passed and the town still did not seem to have surrendered, the irate and impatient CO of the battalion drove himself to the German general's chateau.

Here he noticed a large number of bemedalled officers waiting around for something or another. Descending from his jeep he approached one of them and asked: 'You a colonel?'

When the German answered in the affirmative, the CO pointed to a bemedalled resplendent figure who

seemed to be the centre of the activity and asked. 'Well, who's that character over there?'

'That's the lieutenant-general,' came the answer.

'Well, tell him to hop into this jeep and I'll take care of him,' the battalion commander ordered and closed the 'formal' surrender ceremony in a very abrupt manner. The advance went on, with the First Army thrusting vigorously for the town of Hagen, located due south of Dortmund, where soon they would link up with the Ninth Army. The fighting meanwhile still continued in and around the city of Dortmund, where positions such as the airfield changed hands time and time again in attack, counter attack and then attack once more. By 12th April the great pincer that XVI Corps was forging around Dortmund was nearly completed when it drove prongs about the metropolis to within four miles of each other while the Germans fought desperately to keep open an escape route.

On that day the 75th Division contained the city to the west, cleared Witten to the south west and continued to advance over difficult terrain and against heavy opposition. At the same time the 95th Division entered the north and north eastern edges of the stricken city and continued its advance through rubbled streets made doubly dangerous by mines and German snipers. While mortars and artillery pounded the American rear areas from positions south of the River Ruhr, the infantry worked their way cautiously through the ruined suburbs.

Jeeps raced up and down, carrying out wounded and bringing in ammunition. Shells came roaring in, bringing down what was left of the houses in a thunder of rubble. Fighting continued from street to street, with khaki-clad infantrymen falling in the littered streets with sickening regularity as they were hit by snipers' bullets. Everywhere the windows were boarded up, but the suddenly suspicious infantry were sure that each blind facade hid another sniper; there were enough crumpled khaki-clad figures in the gutters to indicate that. Angrily they burst into the cellars of the ruined houses and ordered out the protesting civilian inhabitants, old men and women, at bayonet point. In some places no quarter was given nor expected. The advance continued.

And then finally on the evening of 13th April, 1945 it was over. In one final burst of energy, the 75th and 95th Divisions pushed forward and cleared the city. The 95th Division's 379th Regiment drove on hurriedly to capture the high ground east of the city which overlooked the Ruhr. This move cut off any possibility of escape for whatever scattered resistance might be left in the smoking ruins of the dead city.

At last after over a week of bitter fighting it was all over in the Ninth Army's sector of the Ruhr, apart from minor pockets here and there, such as that around the city of Dusseldorf. Everywhere the firing began to die away and an echoing silence descended upon the ruined cities of this once prosperous area, the one-time 'workshop of the Reich'. Dazed, dirty and bewildered citizens began to emerge from the cellars to fetch water and view what was left of their ruined homes. GIs relaxed and slung their weapons for the first time in days. The artillery, that every present background music to a war, stopped firing at last. It was all over.

That night, General Fritz Bayerlein of the LIII Corps, received an urgent message from a distraught Model, who had lost contact with virtually all his units, to break out of the Ruhr with everything still available. The order was never acknowledged, answered or obeyed. The next day Fritz Bayerlein, a realist who knew when he was beaten, surrendered.

Below: Infantry hug the wall, sheltering from artillery barrage in Dortmund
Right: One of the millions of homeless

The end

On 13th April Hitler called Model's brilliant young operations officer, Colonel Günther Reichhelm, and told him he was now to be General Wenck's Chief of Staff. In the conversation that followed, the Führer told Reichhelm. 'The Twelfth Army must drive a wedge between the English and American troops and reach Army Group B. They must go all the way to the Rhine!'

Reichhelm who had just come from the utter confusion and nearly complete breakdown of the Ruhr force did not attempt to enlighten the Leader. Keeping his opinions to himself, he listened while Hitler told him that he and Wenck should steal a trick from the Russians. 'They filter in through our lines at night with little ammunition and no baggage.' Then he suggested that Reichhelm should collect a couple of hundred *Volkswagens* and use them to filter through the American lines at night and create such havoc in the enemy's rear that it would be relatively easy for the main

body of the Twelfth Army to follow them and make the decisive breakthrough.

Reichhelm was not convinced. Nor was Model when he heard the news. He did not even bother to pass on the optimistic messages coming from Berlin to his troops. He knew that Wenck would never be able to break through to him. He was reduced to a handful of units, crammed into an area only thirty miles in diameter, with food and supplies sufficient only for three days. When the death of President Roosevelt was announced Hitler was transformed by the news which coincided with the date, Friday the thirteenth (it was received one day after the event in Germany), and he dictated a message to Jodl for Model, which read: 'Troops in the Ruhr are ordered to gather in small groups and hold out as long as possible. Groups which cannot hold their ground must withdraw, reorganise and harass the enemy's rear.' But Model's mood was unchanged. In fact, it was so obvious

A 40mm gun position guards the Elbe pontoon bridge

that the situation was hopeless on that Friday that Model's new Chief of Staff, General Carl Wagener, told Model he should request permission from Berlin to surrender. Such a request from a man of Model's reputation and calibre might convince the High Command that Germany should stop the war at once.

'I could hardly make such a proposal,' Model replied. The idea of surrender was repugnant to him, but as that long grim April Friday drew to a close he knew that the end was near. On that same afternoon he received the information that the Americans were already beginning to cross the Elbe.

The Americans of General White's 2nd Armored had actually crossed the night before in a strength of two armoured infantry battalions at the small town of Westerhusen, south of Magdeburg. By first light the next morning another battalion had joined them and was busily digging in as the

word flew back to General Simpson 'We're across!'

Wenck learned of the crossing almost as soon as Simpson. He acted at once. Although his young cadets were green, they were enthusiastic and eager for the battle that lay ahead. Quickly he sent mobile combat groups of the *Scharnhorst, Potsdam* and *von Hutten* divisions down to the bridgehead, where the Americans were frantically trying to throw a bridge across the river. As Wenck's artillery destroyed the American pontoon bridge, the eager young cadets struck the 2nd Armored positions on the eastern bank of the river with an élan that had been missing from the German army for many a month. Led by armour, the Germans overran the first companies. Colonel Anderson commanding the infantry called frantically for the 2nd's artillery across the river to come to his aid. But the attack had come in so fast that even as the artillery opened up, Anderson knew it was too late; the Germans were already in his positions.

Further up the line American witnesses reported seeing German tanks using American prisoners to shield them while they fired into the American line. The Americans returned the fire with their bazookas. But the range was too great. The bombs simply bounced off the German Mark Vs, and the Americans were forced to withdraw.

The men of the 2nd Armored started to pull back everywhere, though one company holding a group of houses held on to its positions, and called for artillery to 'throw it right on our positions as our men are in the cellars of the houses'. Air strikes were called for but only a few fighter bombers turned up in the course of the whole dawn to noon battle. The fighter landing fields were so far behind the lines that the planes had been forced to carry extra petrol tanks in their wings which meant they could not carry bombs.

In the end General Hinds of the 2nd, who was commanding the operation, recalled his men back across the Elbe. The operation had cost the division 304 men dead and ended its hope of having a bridgehead across the Elbe. In thirty months of combat, it was the first time that the 2nd Armored Division had suffered a real defeat. General Wenck's men had performed a good job of work and he had reason to be proud of them.

The Ninth Army still had a single bridgehead in the 83rd Division's sector at Barby, which constituted a definite threat to Wenck's front but the Commander of the Twelfth Army was no longer concerned with the Americans. He knew that even if Lucht's Eleventh Army could continue to hold out, which seemed likely in the rugged terrain of the Harz, there was not an earthly chance of him crossing the Elbe in strength, breaking through to Lucht, and from his positions in the Harz launching an attack to link up with Army Group B. Model's fate was finally sealed. It could only be a matter of days now.

Although Model had no details of

Brigadier-General John H Hinds

Wenck's limited success on the Elbe, he knew that the skilled young general would never be able to break through to him in spite of Hitler's promises. But he was still not prepared to surrender, even though the enemy was only a matter of kilometres away from his own headquarters.

That enemy was General Ridgway, commander of the XVIII Airborne Corps, fighting as infantry in the Ruhr. On the 15th April, when his command was a bare two miles away from Model's HQ, tough, hooked-nose Ridgway ordered a staff officer, Captain Brandstetter, who spoke fluent German, to go to Model under a flag of truce. He was to tell Model that further resistance was senseless and could result only in needless slaughter. Brandstetter returned with one of Model's staff officers, who gave the field-marshal's answer. In effect it was that he could not consider any surrender proposal and that he was bound by an oath of loyalty to Hitler to fight to the end. Even the mere consideration of Ridgway's suggestion violated his sense of honour as a German officer.

Ridgway decided to make one more try. He sat down and composed a

Above: **AA protection for the Elbe crossing.** *Below:* **Entering Magdeburg**

General Ridgway

personal letter to Model, which read in part as follows: 'Neither history nor the military profession records any nobler character, any more brilliant master of warfare, any more dutiful subordinate of the state, than the American General, Robert E Lee. Eighty years ago this month, his loyal command reduced in numbers, stripped of its means of effective fighting and completely surrounded by overwhelming forces, he chose an honorable capitulation. This same choice is now yours. In the light of a soldier's honor, for the reputation of the German Officer Corps, for the sake of your nation's future lay down your arms at once. The German lives you will save are sorely needed to restore your people to their proper place in society. The German cities you will preserve are irreplaceable necessities for your people's welfare.'

Brandstetter once more returned to Model's HQ to deliver this dignified and moving appeal to the little field-marshal's honour and sense of responsibility, while Ridgway waited impatiently. He returned with Model's Chief of Staff, Wagener. The two men informed Ridgway that it was no use. Field-Marshal Model would not consider any plea whatsoever. Model's Chief of Staff was a wiser man. Ridgway told him he could go back under a flag of truce to take his chance 'in the disaster that was sure to come'. Or he could stay behind at Ridgway's CP and become a prisoner of war. The German general did not debate the issue very long. He chose to stay. Thus Ridgway washed his hands of Model. As he notes in his memoirs: 'That was that. I could do no more. From now the blood was upon Model's head.'

On the day that General Ridgway made his final demand to Model. the Ruhr Pocket had been divided into several smaller pockets. South of the River Ruhr it was split into two enclaves, the larger one in the west including the cities of Düsseldorf and Wuppertal, while east of the river there was a small 'wandering pocket' which contained the command of the Fifteenth Army (von Zangen) and a larger one west of Kassel.

All these pockets were under attack from both south and east and, in some cases, from the north. But although most of them were still prepared to resist a while longer, that resistance was limited on the 15th mainly to sharp defensive fire, which succeeded only in slowing up the pace of the American advance.

Already mass unauthorised surrenders had begun. General von Waldenburg's proud 116th Panzer Division, which had fought in the west for ten months, gave itself up having finally encountered a trap from which it could not escape. Led by two enlisted men and two officers of the US 8th Armored Division, who had been captured in the bitter fighting around Soest, the Panzer Division marched into captivity. So did that famed

formation the Panzer Lehr Division, which had fought so well in Normandy and the Ardennes. Its commander, his staff and what was left of his battered formation followed their brothers-in-arms into the cage.

The 12th Army Group's special investigation group, T Force, now swarmed everywhere into the German positions to seize scientists, politicians, Nazis and anyone else that Allied Intelligence had noted as being worthy of capture. The younger Krupp was taken as a potential war criminal, as was the man who had eased Hitler's way to power, Franz von Papen, the last Nazi ambassador to Turkey. It was there that he had failed to buy the Allied plan for the invasion of Normandy from the spy Cicero, one of the many bloomers he had made in his long life. Secret weapons and the plans of the newest 'terror weapons' were secured, as well as industrial formulae which would be of use in the rebuilding of the post war western economy. One scientist was found working in his laboratory in Essen, just outside the Krupp plant in the midst of the ruins of the once great city, completely oblivious of the mayhem taking place all about him.

Naturally some of the more adventurous Germans trapped inside the remaining pockets were not willing to surrender even when ordered to. On 17th April General von Mellenthin of the Fifth Panzer Army heard that his commander Colonel-General Harpe was preparing to surrender. Mellenthin was not. With a few resolute comrades he broke through the Allied lines and resting by day and travelling at night, covered 250 miles before he was finally captured at Höxter, on the Weser, sixteen days later on 3rd May. There were probably several thousand less important officers and soldiers who did the same and got away with it.

But now the reduction of the Ruhr Pocket was becoming something of a joke. A couple of service troops of the First Army, wishing to get in the fighting before it was too late, com-

Above Left : The Ruhr in ruins. *Above :* Von Papen (right) with Major-General Anderson (centre) and Lieutenant-General Simpson. *Below :* Alfred Krupp, owner of the Essen complex and Just Dillgart, public utilities magnate

mandeered a German engine and somehow managed to get the diesel locomotive to work. Collecting a few likeminded comrades, they roared down the track south of Wuppertal, capturing surprised Germans all along the way.

That day the Intelligence Officer of the US 311th Infantry Regiment called up the mayor of Wuppertal by phone and asked him if he was prepared to surrender the industrial town which was the final objective of the First Army. The Mayor refused. The Intelligence officer insisted that someone should be able to surrender the town. The mayor agreed and summoned a colonel. The same question was put to him and he replied, like the mayor, that he had no authority to do so. Finally a general was brought to the phone. He said that he could not surrender, as he was attached to

ordnance and was in charge of the rear installation only. 'Sorry,' he said apologetically, 'but I don't have the authority. But how about my surrendering? Will that do?'

It did, and the city with its population of half a million passed into American hands. Later 16,000 prisoners of war were guarded by two American MPs, one armed with a carbine, the other with a sub-machine gun. They were the sole means of authority over the seething mass of field-grey-clad prisoners.

By the end of the 15th April, 1945, Model realised that the will to resist of most of his men was completely broken. Hourly his control of the various large and small pockets still fighting, or at least holding out, was growing weaker. Even his contact with the OKW of the German army depended upon the Harz relay station which was presently under attack by the Americans further to the east. Although the German High Command

Russian armour moves in on Berlin; Joseph Stalin tanks

urged him that day to try to restore his positions in any way he could, he knew that most of his remaining divisions were down to less than 2,000 men and lacked either the artillery or general supplies to do anything more than offer weak resistance to the enemy. Offensive action was completely out of the question.

The situation deteriorated rapidly. On the 16th April ammunition was running dangerously low and weapons of all categories were no longer available to replace those lost in action. Model's forces were completely divided. A small pocket to the east contained the command of the Fifteenth Army which was being attacked from south and east, and a larger pocket to the west contained the command of the Fifth Panzer Army, also being attacked by the Americans from south and east. As for Model he was little better than a fugitive with only minimal control over his scattered beaten units and

with his own staff officers and HQ personnel held ready as a final emergency combat reserve. On that day he heard over the radio that Zhukov had just launched a new offensive in the east. In the middle of the night 22,000 Russian cannon had opened fire on the German lines! Thousands of tanks were rolling into action, followed by scores of Russian divisions. When he heard this news, Model told his senior intelligence officer, who was going to remain loyal to him to the last, 'This is the end. It's the smash-up.'

He now realised that the final stage of the plan he had thought up to avoid the shame of surrender would soon have to go into operation. On the previous day he had decreed that all the young and old men in his command should be discharged and return home as civilians at once. This action was designed to save their lives and spare them the humiliation of formal surrender. Now that stage was completed, there was another twenty-four hours

to go before the final part of his decree of the 15th would become effective. Then the remaining men under his command would have three choices. They could make their way home; they could surrender individually; or they could try to break out and make their way to the German lines, there to continue the fight.

On the morning of 17th April the unorthodox Model plan went into effect and the battered remnants of Army Group B ceased to exist by a single stroke of the pen, though here and there some small formations would continue to fight in spite of the Field-Marshal's decree. That morning Model turned to a staff officer and said, 'Have we done everything to justify our actions in the light of history? What is there left to a commander in defeat?' He paused and then said, 'In ancient times they took poison.'

Meanwhile the mass surrenders which had begun on the previous day reached a climax. Each American division involved in the fighting found itself taking at least 2,000 and often as many as 5,000 prisoners. One astonished GI started out from Wuppertal with sixty-eight German prisoners and discovered by the time he got to the regimental POW cage that he had 1,200! The 8th Infantry Division, which had by this time fought its way right across the Pocket from south to north took a record number of 50,192 prisoners on the 17th.

Now virtually everywhere the Germans flooded in to surrender, waving handkerchiefs, sheets, tablecloths, shirts, in fact anything white. And with them came those commanders who had dominated the European and African battlefields for years. Bayerlein of the LIII Corps, Lüttwitz of the XLVII Panzer Corps, Harpe, Commander of the Fifth Panzer Army, Denkert, Waldenburg, Lange and the commanders of the 9th, 180th, 190th and 338th Divisionsall surrendered. In the end there were twenty-nine German generals and one admiral enclosed in the American prisoner of

Some of the 10,000 prisoners captured by 99th Infantry Division of First US Army
Overleaf ; the gigantic canvas city prison compounds

Left: An ancient *Volksturm* soldier gives himself up. *Above:* The fleeing remnants of the German army continue to destroy bridges behind them

war cages at the end of the day.

At a cost of less than 10,000 American soldiers killed, wounded and missing, the Ninth and First Armies took an estimated 317,000 prisoners in the Ruhr. Thousands more had been killed in action or vanished on the 15th when Model had issued his amazing 'demobilisation decree'. Even with so many Germans unaccounted for, there were more enemy soldiers in the POW cages, which were usually open fields hurriedly fenced off with a few lengths of barbed wire, than the Russians had captured at Stalingrad or Budapest or the Allies at the end of the North African campaign in Tunis. On the 17th April 1945 all records for the capture of prisoners throughout the whole war were broken.

But still Model was not accounted for. While the Americans mopped up the few remaining pockets of resistance which refused to surrender, the order went out to find the little field-marshal and bring him back alive.

Bradley, who gave the order, recollects in his memoirs; 'Remembering how this chilly Prussian had blocked our advance through the Siegfried Line in September, I told G-2 to give a medal to the man who brought him in.' But the only trace of Model that came out of the Ruhr was a giant Mercedes-Benz staff car, which Ridgway presented to Bradley as having once belonged to the German field-marshal.

For four days after the surrender, Model wandered through the ruins of Ruhr, escaping the patrols sent out to find him, accompanied solely by a few loyal staff officers. Surrender to him was inconceivable. 'A field-marshal,' he said, referring to Paulus who had surrendered at Stalingrad, 'does not become a prisoner. Such a thing is just not possible.'

He answered one of his officers who again brought up the surrender question by saying: 'I simply cannot do it. The Russians have branded me a war criminal, and the Americans would be

The end of the Third Reich

sure to turn me over to them for hanging.'

By the morning of 21st April 1945 he was alone except for his intelligence chief. 'My hour has come,' he told the staff officer. 'Follow me.'

The intelligence officer thought that Model intended to surrender. But he was wrong. Model led him into the deepest part of the forest somewhere near the industrial town of Duisburg. There he drew his pistol out of his holster and the intelligence officer knew what the little field-marshal intended.

'Anything's better than falling into Russian hands,' he told his companion. 'You will bury me here.'

One pistol shot did it. The marshal's aim was true.

Thus the Battle for the Ruhr came to an end, with a tremendous victory for the Allies, at least in terms of territory and prisoners taken. It was a tragedy for the enemy and whatever one may think of the way that Model ended his life, that brave and bold soldier was the only one of the major German commanders to draw the consequences of the German General Staff's blind loyalty to Adolf Hitler and the Nazi ideal. The man who at the height of his power at the beginning of the Ardennes battle on 16th December 1944 called for his soldiers 'not (to) disappoint the Führer and the homeland . . . Advance in the spirit of Leuthen . . . No soldier of the world can be better than we,' knew that the end of the Nazi empire meant that his own life was forfeited too.

Writing of the way he died, General Essame of the British Army has maintained that 'he thus by British standards spoilt what was in fact a magnificent fighting record on both

the Eastern and Western fronts ... All that was necessary now at this final hour was to form his own battle group, if necessary of one man only, and fight on. There were plenty of Allied soldiers only too ready to ensure him a more dignified exit from a stage on which he had played a distinguished if somewhat sinister part.'

Model was not prepared to make such a dramatic gesture. Perhaps he was a realist as well as a brave man. Unlike all his contemporaries, Kesselring, von Rundstedt, and Buschs, he was not prepared to accept the years of confinement and the humiliations of an Allied court. He paid the debt he owed the Thousand Year Reich that day and disappeared from history, without even a simple cross to mark the place of his passing. The man who buried him later stated, 'I am, as far as I know, the only person who knows where his grave is.'

Behind him he left a scene of sordid horror. In the cities of the Ruhr great piles of rubble blocked the streets; twisted lamp standards stood silhouetted grotesquely against a sky still heavy with smoke. The citizens were apathetic and broken, a prey now to the many thousand displaced persons and former prisoners of war from the east who were paying back the debts of many years of humiliation at German hands. Fighting, looting and murder broke out everywhere, with the few remaining unarmed German civilian police powerless to defend their compatriots. Despite the brave spring sunshine that shone during that last week of April 1945, the Ruhr presented a picture of complete, utter collapse unknown anywhere in Western Europe in five-and-a-half years of total war. It was all over. The 'workshop of Germany' lay in ruins.

Conclusion

'Persistent pace and pressure,' the great military theorist Captain Liddell Hart once wrote, 'are the key to success in any deep penetration or pursuit, and even a day's pause may forfeit it.'

In the first week of April 1945, this basic military maxim seems to have been violated by the Allied Supreme Commander General Eisenhower when he ordered General Bradley to make his first priority the double encirclement of the Ruhr. Thereafter, and only thereafter, was Bradley to drive to the River Elbe, from whence he would presumably launch the final Allied offensive against the 'glittering prize' (as Eisenhower himself once called it) of Berlin, the enemy capital.

Today, we know that Eisenhower had already made his controversial decision to halt the main body of his

forces, the US First and Ninth Armies, on the Elbe, there to wait for the Russians to link up with them from the east. But his field commanders did not know this in that first fateful week of April, as they made their plans for the final direction of the campaign now that the Rhine had been crossed in force. Writing on 27th March, perhaps a week after Eisenhower had crystallised his final strategy in his own mind, Montgomery sent the following coded message to the Supreme Commander: 'My tactical headquarters move to north west to Bonninghardt on Tuesday 29th March. Thereafter . . . my headquarters will move to Wesel-Münster -Wiedenbrück-Herford-Hanover-then by autobahn to Berlin, I hope'. Seven days later and six days after Eisenhower had announced his decision to Stalin and Churchill, General Simpson commanding the US Ninth Army still believed that Berlin was the ultimate target. On 4th April he received 12th Army Group's 'Letter of Instructions, No. 20' which ordered him to conduct a two-phase operation. In phase one he was to drive to Hildesheim, about seventy miles from the Elbe. In phase two, he was ordered to 'advance on order to the east . . . exploit any opportunity for seizing a bridge-head over the Elbe and be prepared to continue the advance on Berlin or to the north east.'

The way that Simpson interpreted the order meant that Berlin was his objective. He told his staff officers he planned 'to get an armoured and an infantry division set up on the autobahn running just above Madgeburg on the Elbe to Potsdam where we'll be ready to close in on Berlin.' Jubilantly he told his officers, 'Damn, I want to get to Berlin and all you people right down to the last private, I think, want it too.'

Even as late as 15th April Simpson was still making plans to get to Berlin when he was ordered to fly to General Bradley's headquarters. En route he finalised his scheme to send

General Omar Bradley crosses 'Hodges Bridge' over the Rhine

the 2nd Armored Division and the 83rd Infantry down the autobahn to Berlin once he had returned from Bradley. An unpleasant surprise was waiting for him at Bradley's HQ in Wiesbaden. As soon as he stepped off the plane, Bradley told him frankly: 'I want to tell you right now. You have to stop right where you are. You can't go any farther. You must pull back across the Elbe.'

'Where in hell did this come from?' Simpson protested. 'I could be in Berlin in twenty-four hours.'

Bradley replied 'I just got it from Ike.'

And there the matter ended. All that remained between Simpson's troops and Berlin was, as one somewhat cynical writer has put it, 'Eisenhower himself'.

Eisenhower's original plan for the conduct of the campaign after the Rhine had been crossed envisaged Bradley's Twelfth Army group in the centre having a limited role. The main effort would be borne by Montgomery's 21st Army Group in the north. But after what can only be termed as Bradley's failure in the Ardennes (he had failed to see the possibility of a German attack; there was no contingency plan for a withdrawal if the Germans did attack; and he had no reserves to speak of for this eventuality), the American general had fired his men to great successes. They had gone from victory to victory and by March Bradley was seeking a larger role in the final campaign. Like Montgomery, Bradley wanted the glory of ending the war. But if Eisenhower's original plan was executed, it would mean the kudos of the last victory would to go Montgomery, a man whom Bradley had learned to detest intensely.

It is, therefore, not surprising that on 21st March a document originated in Bradley's headquarters which changed the whole course of the final

strategy. Entitled 'Re-Orientation of Strategy', the memorandum stated that Allied objectives had changed and had rendered 'obsolete the plans we brought with us over the beaches . . . the metropolitan area can no longer occupy a position of importance . . . all indications suggest that the enemy's political and military directorate is already in process of displacing to the 'Redoubt' in lower Bavaria.'

To meet the threat supposedly posed by this mythical 'Alpine Redoubt', in which according to some ill-informed sources the Germans were to make a last-ditch stand, Bradley suggested that his army group should split Germany in two by driving through the country's centre. This suggestion, added to special pleading on Bradley's part for a larger role for his army group and a cable from General Marshall in Washington warning him to avoid inadvertent conflict with Russians advancing from the east, convinced

Left to right: **Dempsey, Bradley, Montgomery, Simpson**

Eisenhower to make his fateful decision of 28th March, 1945. That day in a quite unprecedented manner, he cabled Marshal Stalin the following decision, which at that time was unknown to the Combined Chiefs of Staff, the British or US governments, or even to his deputy, Air-Chief-Marshal Sir Arthur Tedder: 'My immediate operations are designed to encircle and destroy the enemy defending the Ruhr . . . I estimate that this phase . . . will end late in April or even earlier, and my task will be to divide the remaining enemy forces by joining with your forces.'

Thus the fateful 'stop on the Elbe' decision with its significant, far-reaching political implications was made and suddenly the Ruhr gained first rate importance as the major objective of the bulk of the US troops in Europe. Naturally the Ruhr had played an important role in Allied strategic considerations before this time, but although Eisenhower had all along favoured some sort of a double encirclement of the Rhur, he had still considered Montgomery's intended drive along the northern lip of the great industrial area towards Berlin as the basis of his post-Rhine strategy. Now suddenly the Ruhr itself became the primary objective, with the drive from the Remagen bridge playing an equal role with that from the Rhine around Wesel. As Eisenhower wrote after the war in his *Crusade in Europe:* 'The first step in this movement (the final destruction of Germany) remained the encirclement of the Ruhr. This had always been a major feature of our plans and there was nothing in the situation now facing us to indicate any advantage in abandoning the purpose. On the contrary, it now appeared that this double envelopment would not only finally and completely sever the industrial Ruhr from the remainder of Germany but would result in the destruction of one of the major forces still remaining to the enemy . . . A natural objective beyond the Ruhr was Berlin. It was politically and pyschologically important as the symbol of remaining German power. I decided, however, that it was not the logical or the most desirable for the forces of the Western Allies.'

Due to the pressures created by the flood of protests that stemmed from the British side when it became known that the Allies would halt on the Elbe, Eisenhower was forced to concede in a telegram to Churchill, 'if at any moment 'Eclipse' (the German collapse or surrender) condition should come about anywhere along the front we would rush forward . . . and Berlin would be included in our important targets.' It was as far as the Supreme Commander would commit himself. Yet even this concession might have been realised if the conduct of the operations against the Ruhr had been carried out differently once the two armies, the First and

Ninth, had linked up at Lippstadt.

Kesselring, Eisenhower's opposite number on the enemy side and a skilled strategist, immediately perceived what Eisenhower should do now that the men of Model's Army Group B had been trapped by the 2nd April junction. Writing about the decision to hold the Ruhr, ordered by the German High Command in Berlin, he points out in his memoirs: 'The OKW may have thought a break-out had no longer any prospect of success, and that an encircled Army Group might pin down enough enemy troops to prejudice a strong eastward drive. They may possibly also have believed that the Army Group could be rationed by the Ruhr and that greater supplies could thus be fed to the other units at the front.

'In fact, however, there was only enough food in the Ruhr to feed the troops of both Army group and population for at the most two or three weeks. From a strategic point of view the Ruhr had no interest for Eisenhower; his objective lay far to the east. The only hope of pinning down strong investment forces lay in a stubborn and indeed aggressive defence, which, judging by what I had seen, was not on the face of it likely.'

In fact, Kesselring, who in the past had enjoyed the reputation of being an officer who could 'sense' the enemy's intention and had built up a great reputation as a defensive specialist on this sixth sense, completely misjudged Eisenhower's strategic intention when he concluded 'the Ruhr was not at that moment an American objective and that the British Second and the American Ninth Armies would continue their operations in a northeasterly and easterly direction, that is that they would by-pass the Ruhr'.

Kesselring was wrong. Instead, on the day that the two US armies linked up at Lippstadt and Hitler himself admitted in a 'private talk' that the total defeat of Germany was not only possible but probable, Eisenhower took the Ninth Army away from

Montgomery and committed it, in great part, to the fighting in the Ruhr.

The result was twofold. Montgomery, weakened considerably by the lack of the fifteen divisions of the Ninth Army, found his progress along the northern route slowed down. American and British strategists had regarded this route as the most favoured way to the 'heart of Germany', i.e. the German capital and administrative centre. In spite of intense and uncharacteristic urgency and drive on the part of the 'set battle' British commander, his men had neither the élan nor the weight (two things possessed very definitely by the US Ninth Army) to make a high speed dash to and across the Elbe, which might have forced Eisenhower's hand and made him yet reconsider his decision not to advance to Berlin. Montogomery's progress was so relatively slow against the enemy's determined attempt to keep an escape route open from east to west and across the Elbe, in order to allow soldiers and civilians to escape to the west from the advancing Russians, that he only managed to reach the Baltic and thus prevent the Red Army penetrating into Denmark

Kesselring on 15th May 1945

by a matter of hours.

In addition, eighteen American divisions, including two vitally needed armoured divisions, became involved in the reduction of the Ruhr Pocket for a matter of two weeks when their added weight might have turned the balance and brought the two American armies not only to the Elbe but across it in force a week before they finally reached the river which was the last barrier to Berlin in the west. In the end all that these two mighty armies succeeded in doing was to secure a handful of bridgeheads at combat command strength and even one of these was thrown back in a bloody reversal. Naturally it could be argued that if the Ninth and First Armies had gone all out for the Elbe, leaving only holding forces on both sides of the Ruhr Pocket, the Germans trapped within it would have presented a very real danger to their long lines of communication. But as we have seen, all Model's attempts to break out of the Pocket were repulsed with relative ease, and Kesselring himself has remarked on the lack of offensive spirit on the part of both Army Group B and its commander. Time and time again Model seems to have regarded orders from above, which tried to bolster up his morale and offensive spirit, as being out of touch with the real situation within the Pocket. In fact, Model's attitude right from the day the Allies crossed the Rhine could be summed up in two words: fatalistic and apathetic.

Consequently it would seem that it would not have been beyond the power of the Allies to leave the Ruhr contained by second line troops or some of those inexperienced divisions present in Europe in sufficient numbers by that time, dug in at the Rhine-Herne Canal in the west and the Sieg in the south. With most of Simpson's and Hodges' veteran divisions racing for the Elbe and beyond, the Ruhr would probably have fallen of its own accord due to starvation and lack of morale helped along by the overwhelming weight of the Allied bombing fleets which at this time were crying out for some sort of a mission.

General Patton, Commander of the American Third Army, had taken such chances time and time again during the 1944–1945 campaign, leaving his flanks completely exposed against the kind of opposition present in the Ruhr and sending his armoured columns far out into enemy territory without any flank protection at all. One has only to think in this context of his spectacular two hundred mile dash across Brittany with his 4th and 6th Armored Divisions. Admittedly Simpson and Hodges were no Pattons, but they had under their command enough divisional generals such as White of the 2nd Armored or Rose of the 3rd, who were embued with the same dashing cavalry spirit as the flamboyant commander of the Third Army. Patton's answer to subordinate commanders anxious about their unguarded flanks invariably was his simple bold motto: 'Let the enemy worry about the flanks!'

When the Ninth Army reached the

Above: Patton. *Right:* Complete conquest; US troops relax

Elbe on 11th April 1935, the plea was put forward again that the Elbe should be crossed in force and the drive to Berlin continued. But again Eisenhower stood firm, supported by superiors such as Marshall and subordinates such as Bradley. It was he who advised Eisenhower that the capture of Berlin would cost the US Army 'a hundred thousand casualties . . . to break through from the Elbe to Berlin . . . a pretty stiff price to pay for a prestige objective.' This was when the Germans in the west had been decisively defeated. One can only conclude that Bradley's advice to Eisenhower was motivated by personal reasons. If the Allies were to drive to Berlin, that drive would be commanded by Montgomery who would need not only the US Ninth Army, but other American formations, probably from Patton's Third Army, which were racing against nominal opposition towards the mythical Alpine Redoubt. A drive towards Berlin would mean, in other words, that Bradley would be reduced to conducting a sideshow operation, with the detested Montgomery earning the laurels of the final victory.

Eisenhower, for his part, was not

motivated by such personal, nationalistic reasons. He felt that his position
on the Elbe was not as secure as many
people believed. Writing to the Combined Chiefs of Staff three days after
Simpson had reached the Elbe, he
reported: 'The essence of my plan is to
stop on the Elbe and clean up my
flanks.' A day later he explained his
reasons in a further signal to the same
group. 'While it is true that we have
seized a small bridgehead over the
Elbe, it must be remembered that
only our spearheads are up to the river;
our center of gravity is well back of
there.'

Eisenhower thus added a further
dimension to the great debate, the
question of logistics. But here one
must say with all fairness that if there
were logistic difficulties they were of
his own making. He had allowed his
armies to sprawl in the old discredited
'broad front' strategy and dissipated
his strength. More than forty divisions had crossed the Rhine by the 1st
April, but only eight were positioned
north of the Harz Mountains on the
direct road to Berlin. South of these
mountains there were, counting the
Seventh Army, a total of thirty-one
American divisions, many of which
were engaged in the pointless reduction of the Ruhr Pocket which went on
until April 18th and Harz, which finally
fell on April 22nd. The striking power
and logistical capacity for a major
advance were available that April.
Unfortunately, in the opinion of
Winston Churchill, they were in the
wrong place and heading in the wrong
direction.

In the end the Ruhr became a battlefield between eighteen American
divisions and twenty- one enemy
formations which resulted in the
capture of about 4,000 square miles of
enemy territory, the destruction of
the Germans' major industrial centre
and the withdrawal of 320,000 soldiers
from the German order of battle. This

was achieved at a cost of 2,452 fatal
casualties for the Ninth Army and a
slightly larger number for the First
Army.

In terms of men taken prisoner and
territory captured, it was a cheap
victory, one of the cheapest of the
whole war for the Allies. But it was a
hollow victory.

It did not end the war any more
rapidly nor did it have that supreme
psychological effect on the Germans
that the fall of Berlin at that time

would have done. When the heated discussion between the British and the Americans over the controversial Eisenhower decision to stop at the Elbe was at its height, Churchill made one last desperate appeal to convince Roosevelt of the vital importance of the enemy capital as the immediate strategic and political objective of April 1945. In a cable to the American President, he stated: 'Nothing will exert a pyschological effect of despair upon all German forces of resistance equal to that of the fall of Berlin. It will be the supreme signal of defeat to the German people.'

Because that warning was not heeded, the war continued a further five weeks and with it a further loss of valuable Allied lives and material after the date of that historic link-up of the two victorious American armies at the little German town of Lippstadt.

But more important perhaps than the fact that the war went on longer than was necessary, was that the prolonged battle in the Ruhr, with its important bearing on the campaign that might have been carried out east of the River Elbe, indirectly contributed to the changed face of Western Europe after 1945; the most important and far-reaching rearrangement of territory this century.

Eisenhower himself realised the intimate link between the reduction of the Ruhr Pocket and any campaign he might conduct on the other side of the River Elbe when he wrote to the Chief of Staff in Washington, General Marshall on 6th April stating: 'You must expect now a period in which the lines on your map will not advance as rapidly as they did during the past several weeks. We must pause to digest the big mouthful we have swallowed in the Ruhr area.' When his leading divisions reached the Elbe they showed by the speed of their advance and their lack of casualties that Bradley's estimate of 100,000 casualties was ludicrous. But Eisenhower could still justify his decision to halt by the problem of supplies and the 'big mouthful' he had decided, unnecessarily, to chew in the Ruhr.

General Marshall, Eisenhower's protector and mentor, has called the Battle for the Ruhr 'this unique

victory, won far behind our forward positions and squarely astride our lines of communications'. However, it is my opinion that when military historians come to reassess General Eisenhower's contribution to the 1944-1945 campaign in Western Europe, they will point fairly and squarely to the reduction of the Ruhr Pocket as one of his major strategic blunders. Naturally it is a question of conjecture what might have happened if the Western Allies had not made the Ruhr their major objective of April 1945 and instead had seized Berlin ahead of the Russians. But one cannot doubt that, stiffened by Churchill's resistance to what he visualised as the new danger from the east, the political map of Central Europe would be different from what it is today. Perhaps it is primarily for this reason, the futility of it all, that so little has been written about a great battle which yielded more prisoners than the Russians took at Stalingrad or the Allies at the end of the North African campaign. Historians have recognised the basic pointlessness, in spite of the heroism and self-sacrifice on both sides, of the whole affair.

In the final analysis, the Battle for the Ruhr was a battle which should never have been fought.

Bibliography

A Soldier's Story by Omar Bradley (Eyre & Spottiswoode, London. Holt, Rhinehart and Winston, New York)

Crusáde in Europe by Dwight Eisenhower (Doubleday, New York)

Struggle for Europe by Chester Wilmot (Collins, London, Harper & Row, New York)

The German Army in the West by Siegfried Westphal (Cassell, London. Athenaum Verlag, Frankfurt)

The Memoirs of Field-Marshal Kesselring (Kimber, London. Athenäum Verlag, Frankfurt)

The Last Battle by Cornelius Ryan (Collins, London, Simon & Schuster, New York)

The Last 100 Days by John Toland (Barker, London. Random House, New York)

Company Commander by Charles MacDonald (Ballantine, New York)

Battle for Germany by H Essame (Scriber, New York)